I WILL NOT!
PURSUING THE PATH TO PERSEVERANCE

BISHOP GREG D. GILL
FOREWORD BY REV. RICHARD T. HILSDEN

I WILL NOT! Pursuing the Path to Perseverance

Copyright © 2021 by Bishop Greg D. Gill

Cover designed by Lavdi Designs

ISBN 9798597135939
ISBN 978-1-329-81651-0
Printed in the United States

Published By
AWM Publishing House
PO Box 18043 Shawnessy
PO Calgary AB,
Canada T2Y 0K3
www.awmpublishing.ca

Scriptures taken from the Holy Bible Amplified Bible, Classic Edition (AMPC) Copyright © 1954, 1958, 1962, 1964, 1965, 1987 by The Lockman Foundation. New King James Version (NKJV) Scripture taken from the New King James Version®. Copyright © 1982 by Thomas Nelson. Used by permission. All rights reserved.
New Living Translation (NLT) Holy Bible, New Living Translation, copyright © 1996, 2004, 2015 by Tyndale House Foundation. Used by permission of Tyndale House Publishers, Inc., Carol Stream, Illinois 60188. All rights reserved.
The Holy Bible, English Standard Version. ESV® Text Edition: 2016. Copyright © 2001 by Crossway Bibles, a publishing ministry of Good News Publishers. Copyright © 1992 by American Bible Society.
Copyright © 1995, 2003, 2013, 2014, 2019, 2020 by God's Word to the Nations Mission Society. All rights reserved.
The Christian Standard Bible. Copyright © 2017 by Holman Bible Publishers. Used by permission. Christian Standard Bible®, and CSB® are federally registered trademarks of Holman Bible Publishers, all rights reserved.
King James Version (KJV) Public Domain.
NET Bible® copyright ©1996–2017 by Biblical Studies Press, L.L.C. http://netbible.com. All rights reserved.
Holy Bible, New International Version®, NIV® Copyright ©1973, 1978, 1984, 2011 by Biblica, Inc.® Used by permission. All rights reserved worldwide.
New American Standard Bible®, copyright © 1960, 1971, 1977, 1995, 2020 by The Lockman Foundation. All rights reserved.
Good News Translation (GNT) Copyright © 1992 by American Bible Society
Amplified Bible, Classic Edition (AMPC) Copyright © 1954, 1958, 1962, 1964, 1965, 1987 by The Lockman Foundation

I WILL NOT!
Pursuing the Path to Perseverance

Bishop Greg D. Gill

Endorsements for I Will Not!

Bishop Greg Gill has been my friend since 1995. I have seen him face the challenges of life with a faith that both honors God and brings hope to others. When Bishop writes, "I will not," he is not writing words down from a theological point of view, but he is writing from a testimonial point of view. In other words, he's testifying to God's faithfulness in his life.

    Bishop is telling us from actual difficult experiences he's had to journey through, and yet communicating to anyone going through the "trial of their life," don't give up, God's got this, He's going to see you through! I recommend Bishop Greg Gill's book to anyone struggling to hold on to God. The book is filled with insightful keys that will inspire your faith, provoke you to keep confessing God's promises, and strengthen you to offer songs of praise that will glorify God and uplift your heart.

Pastor Carlos Sarmiento
Orlando House of Prayer

I am delighted that Bishop Greg Gill has written this book, I WILL NOT! and at the same time, I am thrilled and humbled to be part of the endorsement of such a timely release of hope, which will help to ignite bold courage to many. And no matter what life challenges may come, the declaration I WILL NOT! will break forth from many lips and hearts to a victorious end, giving glory to God!

Dr. Glenisaah Deborah
Founder/President, THE FORGE TNT

Over the past 25 years, Bishop Greg Gill has been a regular speaker at our church and has a gift for bringing the Word of God alive in a practical and inspiring way. He now has written a must-read book that will encourage and empower you to not give up or give in. Each chapter is filled with key insights; deeply rooted in Spirit and scripture. Read this book and learn from one of the best teachers of the Word I know.

Pastor Shannon Mischuk
New Song Church and World Outreach

Reading Bishop Greg Gill's book provides a testimony of perseverance. Not a down and dirty trust in yourself, or own perseverance, but a completely undone, God I trust in you alone perseverance. If you've been upset by life's paradox between what you believe and what happens to your life and ministry, this book is for you.

The Bishop's personal story, principles expounded, and foundational truths shared throughout, gives hope to the hopeless and provide a light in the darkness of the pain and despair that come when we perceive destiny as lost. The clear declaration of God's restoration and the keys provided to grab on to for restoring your God-given destiny are well-worth the read.

Dr. D. L. (Doug) Atha
Trinity Western University

There are moments in every person's life that you are pressured with the option to give up, and inevitably there will be at least one moment that you think you don't even have a choice. Bishop has not only been in those woods, but he also cut down the whole forest to build the beautiful life he now enjoys with his beloved Diana and seven children.

This memoir of God's presence sustaining Bishop will invite you to take refuge in its pages and find a respite of lodging for yourself in the Love and Grace God has stored up for you. I WILL NOT! will give you the keys and footing to stand when it's impossible and even forge an amazing life out of the most trying of times. In a pastorally prophetic way, Bishop will not just point you to the path—he'll also show you the footprints of The Savior in his own life, where He carried Bishop through every impossible storm. Don't just read these pages. Linger in them and allow them to linger in you. If there's one book you buy in this season, make it I WILL NOT! by Bishop Greg Gill.

Rev. Warren Beemer
Pastor, Healing Place Church in Boerne, Texas

It was wonderful to read about the journey my dear friend Bishop Greg Gill has gone on. From tragedy to triumph, from a head held low to a head held high. The lessons he learned and Biblical principles he has applied here will help you walk through your valleys with confidence and faith to be the overcomer God created you to be. Well done, Bishop!

Dr. David H. Mischuk
Pastor, New Song Church & World Outreach
President: International Helps Ministries Inc.

If you are inclined to live a mediocre life and settle for the status quo, the message of finding a path to perseverance may just be beyond your understanding and beyond your interest. If, however, you are committed to living a life of faith, adventure, and pursuing God's will in your life, this message will be fuel to your soul. As are all church planters worldwide, we are committed to fulfilling God's will wherever we are. We are always looking for and desiring encouragement and support from people like Bishop Greg Gill and this life-giving message.

It is not easy being a David who will take on the giant, yet we all will face giants whether in the valley of Elah or the hill country of Hebron. There is always an impossible battle awaiting you and standing in front of your promise. There is always an intimidating and taunting giant telling you that you will and cannot succeed.

The message from this book emerges from Bishop's life and will build your perseverance and faith so you won't quit, you will not give up, and you will not be destroyed. Oh, don't get me wrong, there are challenges, difficulties, and some losses, yet this message that we are more than conquerors is truth.

Bishop's message isn't just positive thinking mixed with some popular ideas but is a practical application of God's Word to step into and seize your destiny. This is a read that you will make notes from and apply to your everyday life. When you are finished and applying this message, you will be empowered and propelled forward in your God-designed destiny.

Rev. Harvey Trauter
Pastor, Catalyst and Coach City Axis Leadership

People are willing to improve their circumstances but are unwilling to improve themselves –James Allen. The greatest gap in the world is the space between knowing and doing.

Bishop takes readers on an inspiring and motivational journey from obscurity to a place of fulfilling destiny. A must-read for anyone who wants to bridge the gap between knowing and doing.

Rev. Ben Adekugbe
Pastor, Genesis Life Centre

This book has given me important new insights into our relationship with God. Through I WILL NOT! Bishop Greg Gill has provided strong insight into the spiritual realities of battle, warfare, and victory through the power and presence of God.

Every Christian should take up this book as a weapon of spiritual growth on the battlefield of faith. As the world moves toward ever-increasing crisis and confusion, Bishop lays out the road map for achieving divine fulfillment through acts of faith, love, hope, and dedication. With the heart of an Apostle, he demonstrates the realities of the Christian life and the profound victory that is available to every believer that pursues the plan of Jesus Christ. I WILL NOT! is a war cry for this generation and a rallying point for every believer intent on living wholly for the Lord.

Rev. Jon Sarpong
Pastor, Inspire Church

The book I WILL NOT! By Bishop Greg Gill is a timely book and a book to read in the season we are living in today. As we try to navigate through the inevitable storms of life, the earthquakes of emotional traumas and personal setbacks, or other shock waves of life that can cause us to easily give up—Bishop Gill in this book encourages us to persevere through the Word of God and to never throw in the towel no matter what we may be going through.

In reading this amazing and uplifting book, I must admit that I have been powerfully blessed and uplifted. My life has been impacted and empowered to persevere and declare I WILL NOT! but rather pursue the path of perseverance.

This book is a truly life-changing and life-inspirational book that I strongly recommend to everyone.

Dr. Kazumba Charles Th.D.
Founder/President KiTV TV Network

This isn't just a book or an encouragement from the Bishop. This is a living, breathing, life-giving prophetic exhortation from a powerful man of God. I have journeyed with Bishop Gill through many tough days and through wonderful times as well for over 30 years—that spirit of that incredible journey has been captured in these pages; encapsulated into a succinct and transformative admonition that has brought hope and encouragement to me in a time of need, and I'm certain it will continue to bring hope, joy, and strength to me at this time. I'm sure it will do the same for you. If you have faced giants in your life, consume this book. Filled with the Word of God, it will impact your life for the better as you receive and apply it.

Mark Griffin
Mark Griffin Ministries & Coaching

Acknowledgments

I am a worshiper at heart and a minister of the Word. Being an author was not something I thought of. I have had many people encourage me to write a book through prophetic word and friends in the ministry.

Rev. Rick and Judy Hilsden have known me since I was very young and gave me my first opportunity to pastor right out of Bible college. They have seen me through the ups and downs that I talk about in this book, taught, believed, and cared for me deeply.

Thirty years ago, Hughy Watkins and I through our worship journey together at Bible College, became covenant brothers; our brotherhood has stood the test of time; I'm truly thankful.

Pastor Warren Beemer came into my life just at the right time. We have journeyed through some of the same struggles and have encouraged each other along the way. I'm deeply grateful for his friendship.

Dr. Doug and Shawnee Atha gave me an opportunity when it seemed like ministry was over. They kept believing and loving me, and to this day, they are truly a blessing to my life.

Rev. Andrew and Evelyn Picklyk (Mom and Pops), their unconditional love and frequent check-ins have meant more than they'll ever know.

Pastor Bill Olson listened and cried with me on a regular basis for six years. He later officiated Diana and my wedding ceremony.

Pastor Elhadj Diallo for his love, support, wisdom, friendship and for being a listening ear.

Pastor Jon Sarpong for his daily phone calls, love, support and friendship.

My cousin Rich Janes has stood by my side through thick and thin and would always pick me up off the floor as I went through some of my darkest times. He's my cousin but also one of my closest friends.

To my family who has helped me in many ways throughout my life: Aunt Betty and Uncle Ron, Aunt Dorothy, Uncle Paul, and Aunt Glenna, who always cheer me on and believe in me for big things. Aunt Gail and Aunt Donna for their love, encouragement, and support.

Uncle Kenn and Aunt Cheryl, who believed in me in ministry and were there to help me through a very difficult time.

My Mom and Dad (Sandra and David Gill) helped me through my darkest days, and as much as I did not want to go through what I went through, they walked with me, and I'm truly thankful. As well, my sister Shannon, her husband Neil, and family were also there for me. I'm thankful for their kindness and compassion.

My spiritual father and Bible school professor, Bill Carruthers, taught me how to love the Bible, for which I was able to walk this journey with a firm foundation.

Pastors Andoni and Babette Ros have been a listening ear, a tower of strength, and a sounding board. Their wisdom was a true gift of God.

Pastor Simon Clarence (Mufasa) always seemed to call me at the right time with wisdom and encouragement. I'm thankful for him not giving up on me.

Prophet Ben and Pastor Dee Adekugbe, who saw the vision and encouraged me to write this book: Walking through this journey, including the past fifteen years, has been an honor.

There are many others I'm thankful for, but to name a few: Rob Polkowski, Dan Colantonio, Kevin Kirby, Robbie Galbraith, Pastor Mark and Evelyn Scarr, John W. Lucas III, Pastor Anthony and Madelaine Greco, Dr. Randy Johnson, Kenneth Bay, and Dr. David and Shannon Mischuk.

Finally, to the nations of the world who have accepted me with open arms, allowed me to be a part of their world and to help fulfill the destiny and call God has on my life, thank you!

Greg

Dedication

I am thankful for the opportunity that the Lord Jesus Christ has given me to share some of my journey with the nations of the world and the ability to communicate ideas that will help us practically move forward in life. I know that "without Him, I can do nothing" but "with Him all things are possible."

I dedicate this book to those who have not given up despite the circumstances that they have faced. You have stood strong in the face of adversity, and although you could have given in to pressure, criticism, and circumstance, you have continued to believe that things can get better. You are a champion. You are victorious. You are an overcomer. Your best days are still ahead of you. God still has a plan!

A special thank you to my wife Diana (Lady Di). Your love and encouragement mean more than you will ever know. Each day you cause me to keep going toward the dreams that God has given to me and believe in the call of God on my life. It is my honor to walk with you as my wife and partner in ministry. As I watched you go through the process of writing your own book, you have now encouraged and believed in me to see this book completed.

To my daughters, thank you for giving me the freedom to do what I'm called to do and the sacrifices you make to share your father with others so that I can take the Gospel of The Kingdom to the World.

Also, to all those who have encouraged me and spoken words of life into me, I thank you from the bottom of my heart. Your words have made a difference.

Greg

Table of Contents

Acknowledgments vii

Dedication ix

Foreword 1

The Foundation 5

I Will Not! 17

Anywhere But Backwards 35

God Will Restore You 59

Step into Your God-Given Destiny 65

Seven Steps to a Turnaround 77

Time for Overflow and Abundance 87

Testimonies 91

New Mindset 101

Foreword

In life, there are but a few people who model what it means to truly "walk the talk." You know what I mean! These people endeavor to live out their daily lives by demonstration, not just communication. It's called, in layman's terms, to "practice what you preach." In Bishop Greg Gill's recent book release, *I WILL NOT!* he cleverly marries the two concepts. It combines teaching with a practical way to live it out in our daily lives.

I WILL NOT! is a faith-filled book. As you read it, you will find it will inspire you to believe God for the impossible, the improbable, and the unlikely to happen.

Within its pages, you will discover that a happy life is simply a decision, a choice you must make. Life is full of struggles, as you will witness when you read, but it is how you respond to the struggles that make the difference.

Do you have a dream? This book outlines the path to accomplish it! Never, never, never give up! Allow me to quote him, "God always has a way. The very place where I was rejected is where God used to restore me."

Our Personal Connection

Bishop Greg and I go back to a point when I was the Kid's Camp Director, and he was a camper. From that day on, I saw great potential in this very young man. As a result, I have continued to observe him through his years of youth and college. Upon graduation, he joined me on the team where he became the Youth and Creative Arts Pastor, and I was the Lead Pastor. He often reminds me that those days were marked as the "good ole days."

Since then, we have remained close friends. I have been with him through many seasons of life, both the ups and downs. The book you're about to read goes into it all in-depth.

It gives me a great privilege to write this foreword to his first book *I WILL NOT!* I am confident that the reader will thoroughly enjoy the read. It will challenge you to get all that God wants from you and, in return, receive the blessings that are in store for all believers! *I WILL NOT!*

Rev. Richard T Hilsden
President, Wind & Wave Ministries

He [God] Himself has said, I will not in any way fail you *nor* give you up *nor* leave you without support. [I will] not, [I will] not, [I will] not in any degree leave you helpless *nor* forsake *nor* let [you] down, (relax My hold on you)!

[Assuredly not!]

(Hebrews 13:5b AMPC)

Chapter 1

The Foundation

I grew up in Brockville, Ontario, Canada, for the first 17 years of my life, with my parents and younger sister. Coming from a home where hospitality was very important, I learned the art of hospitality at a young age. When I was about two or three years old, I would talk to family and friends at church and invite them to our house for coffee without my parents being aware. I would say, "Come in for coffee!". To this day I still love visiting people over coffee.

At three years old, I could sing the books of the Bible from beginning to end without hesitation. God was building a foundation for me even at a young age.

When our pastor's son had a tragic accident, we had an interim pastor, Ken Bombay. He brought revival nights to our church as he sang old-school hymns from the piano. My mom told me that I would stand in the front pews and watch him play, all the while jumping up and down and clapping my hands. I would sneak up to the piano and sit right on the piano bench

The Foundation

with him! The love of the altar was born in me, and it's still my favorite place to be and feel the presence of God.

At seven years old, I remember giving my heart fully to Jesus at Lakeshore Pentecostal Camp in Cobourg, Ontario, which I had attended every summer since I was nine months old. The next day I was also filled with the Holy Spirit at the children's tabernacle. These are some of the many transforming moments that are very dear to my heart.

In my grade five yearbook, all the pictures of the students were black and white and had no printed names under the picture like they do now. I had handwritten the names of the students underneath their photos so I would remember who they were. I still have this book today, and it's like I was doing Facebook way back then before Facebook was a thing.

The importance of staying connected to friends was evident at a young age. Throughout my growing up years, I would have many pen pals to write to, and I would have boxes and boxes of letters from friends. Now we have email and Facebook messenger to keep us connected.

The Bible was an important part of my growing up as well. Growing up in a Christian home, I was taught the value of following it every day. We would have family devotions before school at 7:30 a.m. sharp. If I wasn't at the table before, I would have to wait till after devotions to eat breakfast. Again, these moments are a part of the foundation that God was building in me through my parents.

In my teenage years, I attended the youth ministry in our church, and I only had one youth pastor, who was the assistant pastor - Pastor Steve and Ann Kohls. Today, after all these years, they are still very close to my parents. They are wonderful people and really believed in me, always giving me

The Foundation

an opportunity to be used in ministry at an early age. I was leading worship in my youth group, and I was invited to minister to many different youth ministries. As I had this opportunity leading worship, people saw the call of God on my life at an early age and always told me, "You're going to be a pastor." I usually argued with them, though, because in my mind and heart, I wanted to be a radio announcer. I said unless God really calls me, I'm going to continue on the path toward radio. When I was in high school, still looking toward radio or sports announcer, I was the voice of my high school. I was the one that did all the track meets, football games and made all the announcements for the whole school.

In 1986 my family decided we would go on a trip to Vancouver to go to Expo 86 and my cousin's wedding. Before we went, I attended Ottawa Valley Camp, and my parents were to pick me up, and we would start our trip from there. While I was at the camp, I felt the call of God on my life, and I committed myself to go into full-time ministry. I couldn't deny it anymore from what others had spoken over me in my growing up.

I told my parents all about it, and then we went on our trip. I was excited to go and see western Canada as I had not been there before. I would be able to see all of my cousins and couldn't wait to be with them. Family was very important growing up, as we spent many holidays together.

When I returned home, I continued seeking God as to what I was to do after high school. While I went to sleep, I would listen to a sermon of Sam Farina every night to the point of my Mom memorizing it! Listening to Hiram Joseph sing and worship music from Integrity's Hosanna Music always helped me go to sleep.

The Foundation

For my eighteenth birthday, my mom threw me a birthday party at the church with all my friends. While the party was going on, my friends made me go up and sing like Hiram Joseph, which I would sometimes do, and mimic him. In the middle of the song, the real Hiram Joseph walked into the room and grabbed the mic! I fell to the ground! I couldn't believe it. What a surprise!

I did follow that call from youth camp, and it took me to Peterborough, Ontario, where I went to Eastern Pentecostal Bible College for four years. It was during this time that I developed lifelong friendships I still have to this day. My biblical studies were taught by many amazing men of God who knew the Word. One of the professors was Bill Carruthers, who would become my spiritual father, who taught me to write in my Bible and make notes all over it. His teaching of the Word has helped me all throughout my years, and I draw from his teachings still to this day.

I had the opportunity to intern at a church in Calgary, Alberta, in 1991 for two and a half months. It was during this time I believed I would return to Calgary one day to minister. I wrote this in my journal in November of 1991.

In the final year of Bible college, I drove back and forth from Peterborough to Bowmanville, where I helped lead worship at a youth ministry there with Pastor Steve Sparling. In January, Pastor Rick Hilsden, the lead pastor at the time, told me he'd like me to consider coming on staff at the church. In February, I started to lead worship part-time at the youth ministry and then serve in the church and also lead some worship for Sunday service. After graduation in April, I started ministry at Liberty Pentecostal Church in Bowmanville, Ontario, on May 1st. I was feeling very blessed that I had a

The Foundation

position even months before most people even graduated. Shortly after that, I was married, and together, we pastored at the church. I was taught much of what I use today in ministry during the five and a half years I was at this church as the Minister of Youth and Creative Arts and then Worship and Evangelism. During this time, I developed a very deep bond with both Lead Pastor Rick Hilsden and Associate Pastor Mark Scaar, which I still enjoy today.

In the summer of 1997, I was asked to speak at a youth retreat and meet the leadership team for a church in Calgary, Alberta, for a weekend in September. In July 1997, I led worship for a youth camp at Ottawa Valley Camp, and the camp speaker was Carlos Sarmiento. He shared with me that while I was practicing for the worship that night, he heard the word AL-BER-TA and asked me if it meant anything to me. Carlos, being from the United States, was not familiar with Canadian provinces, as this was his first trip to Canada. I said, "Whoa! Does that mean anything to me? Right now, I've been praying about going to Calgary, ALBERTA, as I have an opportunity to go on a pastoral team at a church there." I couldn't believe it—confirmation from the Lord.

My first daughter Meghan was born in October, and by the end of December, my family had moved to Calgary where I pastored the youth and young adult ministry for five and a half years. In that time, I also helped a ministry called Tehillah Monday, which was one of the leading-edge ministries in the nation for young adults and youth. I piloted a conference called Fire in the Rockies, which brought youth ministers from around the nation to be poured into and equipped. By this time, two more daughters, Carly and Brianna were also born.

The Foundation

In 2003, finally, my dream to pastor my own church in Calgary came to pass. In September, Destiny Christian Centre International was birthed in a movie theatre, which was interesting because, growing up, I was not allowed to go to one. For our opening service, my parents were there, and I noted that I hadn't been allowed to go to a theater, but now, I had a church in one.

We thrived as a church, and many lives were touched by his Holy Spirit and saved. I also began to do Ignite Conferences which involved many speakers that came to share the Word of God. Powerful anointed men of God and the Holy Spirit would always show up and pour out. In 2006, a moment I remember and must share is when Sammy Rodriguez spoke a word over me at the conference.

"Stand with me one more time. Aim your anointing toward them. (Then he spoke in tongues). Go throughout this nation, man of God! Go throughout this nation, with the anointing of the horn and not the flask. Go throughout this nation like Samuel. Call out the Davids! Call out the Davids! For the Lord has placed an anointing of Samuel upon you as a prophet to go throughout this nation and call out the Davids. God has anointed you to call out the Davids, and they will be under your tutelage under your mentoring. They will prosper. They will thrive. They will learn what a true covenant relationship is. They will learn about holy and righteous living. They will see and will grow, and you will share your victories and your pains, and they will learn to fight against the bear and the lion before they defeat the Goliaths and the Absaloms. Go! Go!

"Under the anointing of Samuel. With the anointing of the horn, anoint the Davids of Canada, Thailand, Asia, and the

The Foundation

Nations! Go! Go! Go, go now, go now. And the Lord says unto you, as you bless the others and as you travel and call out the Davids, I will take care of the church. I will grow as you grow others; I will grow that which is yours as you go out there and grow that which is mine. Be ye not afraid for provision is here right now. For new strength is here right now, and nothing will be able to stand in your way. Nothing will be able to stand in your way. Give the Lord a praise offering!"

I listened to this word over and over again. I received it and believed God for it.

In 2006, my fourth daughter Jessica was born, but by 2008, my life had turned upside down as I went through a marriage separation, and eventually had to close the church I had dreamed of and felt like I was starting over. I didn't know where to go or what to do. I remembered the word that was spoken over me. I knew my God was still with me, and I knew I could not give up.

The Foundation

9 months old

2 years old

Grade 5 Year Book
10 years old

14 years old

*People come into our lives
for a reason, a season, or a lifetime.*

Author Unknown

Chapter 2

I Will Not!

I was sitting in my office one day, and the Lord dropped this phrase in my heart, "I will not." Have you ever told anybody that before? I will not do that; I will not clean my room; I will not do those dishes. Do you know what I am talking about?

The phrase "I will not" can be seen as unfavorable, refusing to do something, but it can also be seen in a positive light when you refuse to give up no matter how bad things get and how tough the road is.

I Will Not Go Down!

In life, some people would like to see you go down, give up, and quit. They want to see you fail, to be miserable, to throw in the towel, hide, and never come out again into the light. That is the plan of the enemy, to use people to get you to quit. But God's plan for you is not to fail, not to quit, not to throw in the towel, but for you to succeed. It does not mean you will not go through tough times in this world. You will have trouble; the world is filled with troubles on every side. The Bible says in

I Will Not!

John 16:33 (NET), "I have told you these things so that in me you may have peace. In the world you have trouble and suffering, but take courage—I have conquered the world."

The focus of the enemy is to see us fail.

The goal and focus of the enemy of our soul are to see us fail by bringing trouble. Still, he cannot win because we are overcomers in Jesus's name. John 10:10 (NIV) says, "The thief comes only to steal and kill and destroy; I have come that they may have life, and have it to the full." The enemy plans to get you out of the picture. To make sure you never amount to anything and see that you fail at everything you do in life.

There are Giants in the Way!

Now the Philistines gathered their forces for war and assembled at Sokoh in Judah. They pitched camp at Ephes Dammim, between Sokoh and Azekah. Saul and the Israelites assembled and camped in the Valley of Elah and drew up their battle line to meet the Philistines. The Philistines occupied one hill and the Israelites another, with the valley between them.

A champion named Goliath, who was from Gath, came out of the Philistine camp. His height was six cubits and a span. He had a bronze helmet on his head and wore a coat of scale armor of bronze weighing five thousand shekels; on his legs, he wore bronze greaves, and a bronze javelin was slung on his back. His spear shaft was like a weaver's rod, and its iron point

I Will Not!

weighed six hundred shekels. His shield bearer went ahead of him. Goliath stood and shouted to the ranks of Israel, "Why do you come out and line up for battle? Am I not a Philistine, and are you not the servants of Saul? Choose a man and have him come down to me. If he is able to fight and kill me, we will become your subjects; but if I overcome him and kill him, you will become our subjects and serve us." Then the Philistine said, "This day I defy the armies of Israel! Give me a man and let us fight each other." On hearing the Philistine's words, Saul and all the Israelites were dismayed and terrified.

1 Samuel 17:1– 11 NIV

An enormous giant faced the Israelites led by King Saul. Goliath, for forty days with the Philistines, came forward every morning and evening and took his stand and shouted his usual defiance, and whenever the Israelites saw the man, they all fled from him in great fear. They were terrified and dismayed by what they saw and what they heard. It immobilized them. Not one person, including King Saul, was willing to take on the giant. They had no leader, no direction, and strength—they were all incapacitated by the giant that stood in their way.

What others were unable to accomplish, David accomplished with faith and confidence in God.

David, a small inexperienced young boy, just happened to be there when Goliath the giant spoke. He was grieved that not one person was willing to challenge the giant. David was willing because he believed in himself and the God he served. He believed his God could bring down that giant, no matter how big or experienced the giant was. With faith and belief, David said in 1 Samuel 17:26 (NIV), "What will be done for the man who kills this Philistine and removes this disgrace from Israel? Who is this uncircumcised Philistine that he should defy the armies of the living God?" The Israelite soldiers told David the reward the king was offering to anyone willing to fight the giant. David responded by saying to Saul, "Let no one lose heart on account of this Philistine; your servant will go and fight him" (1 Samuel 17:32 NIV). What others were unable to accomplish, David accomplished with faith and confidence in God.

What are Some of Your Giants?

We all have giants in our lives that are staring at us daily, calling out and mocking us.

The Giant of Debt. You say, "Well, I am in debt; I am in debt so much, I do not know how I will get out." A friend of mine struggled financially for so long. One day, he came to a meeting with me at a gathering of ministers. At the end of the meeting, one of the ministers came up to me and pulled me aside. He told me he felt that he would like to bless my friend who ministered. He said, "I want to write him a check for $100,000." Now, my friend had nothing, and in 30 seconds in that meeting, God spoke and changed his whole life. It is not just about money, but money can help remove some giants in your life.

I Will Not!

The Giants of Sickness and Disease. It is not God's will for you to be sick. God wants you healed, but people do get sick; that is the bottom line, and we cannot deny it. That giant of sickness and disease stares and laughs at you every day and makes you feel sick and tired so that it becomes tough to pray.

The Giant of Lack. You do not have what you feel you should have. That giant of lack tugs at you daily and puts pressure and frustration upon you because of the many things you lack. Even though you daily confess the word of God that says, "My God shall supply all my needs according to his riches in Christ Jesus" (Philippians 4:19 Authors Paraphrase), this giant makes you feel inadequate and that there will never be enough. He brings doubt about the all-sufficient God.

The Giant of Fear. Fear broken down is False Evidence Appearing Real—fear of things that are not even happening! It is said that fear and worry are connected and that 90% of most things we worry about do not even happen.

The Giant of Unsaved Family Members. What about unsaved family members? Is that a giant in your life? You are not sure if they are ever going to come to the Lord.

I met a lady several months ago, and she came to me after the service and said, "Pastor, you need to know that for sixty-five years, I have been praying for my children to come to the Lord. Then just two weeks ago, one of my children dedicated their lives to Jesus. God answered one of those prayers. For sixty-five years, I've been praying, and I never gave up." Can you pray for sixty-five years for something

I Will Not!

without giving up? Can you even pray for one day, one week, one month, or one year without giving up?

Other giants include a Man-Pleasing Spirit. You want to keep everybody happy, but can I tell you that it will lead to challenges. You may be struggling with your walk with the Lord and are not sure what to do. Maybe you are struggling with your future. I do not know what giant you are facing, but I know that all of us face them.

> ***Just because you have giants in your way does not mean that things are over.***

Just because you have giants in your way does not mean that things are over.

Yes, we all have giants, but we need to look at those giants, stare them down and say, "I can defeat these giants! These giants will not defeat me! I will defeat them!"

The giants in your life are the enemies you need to get you to your destiny. You needed to be fired from that job, so you could get to where God wants you to be. You needed to go through that trial, so God could get you where He needed to put you because He has a divine assignment for you. If you did not have giants in your way, you could not be where God wants you to be, and some of us need the giants to step into what God has for us.

Having to fight the giants in your life will not be easy; it will be painful. However, when you overcome and get to the

I Will Not!

other side, you will realize that God permitted the giants and was with you all the while. He was working on your behalf, working behind the scenes when you could not see.

David went from being a shepherd boy to a warrior, and then to a king because he let the giant know that he was going down; he faced and defeated him.

What Giants are you Facing?

The Scripture tells us in 2 Corinthians 4:8–9 (NIV), "We are hard pressed on every side, but not crushed; perplexed, but not in despair, persecuted, but not abandoned; struck down, but not destroyed." What that means is if you are sitting here, you still have life. You are still breathing. There is nothing the enemy can do about it. He has no power over your life unless you give him power.

Many years ago, you would often hear "Come out with your hands up" during the western movies. Today, I want us to take that line and let the enemy know, "Enemy, I am coming out with my hands up because I am praising my Lord."

I am coming out with my hands up.

I am praising God because my praise is more significant than my failure.

How do you Defeat your Giants?

The devil does not have a chance against you! Here are some critical steps to defeating the giants in your life.

1. Stare it down! Let that situation know that God is bigger, stronger, and more powerful.

I Will Not!

2. Speak to it! Declare and decree the word of God into that situation. Job 22:28 (NASB) says, "You will also decide something, and it will be established for you." So speak it into the spirit of the atmosphere and get things moving on your behalf for things to be established.

3. Start giving thanks! Be like David and give a victory cry. Shout it out before it even happens. Envisioning the breakthrough is related to thanksgiving in your heart. Start thanking God for them even before the answers come.

Hebrews 12:2 (KJV) says, "Jesus, the author and finisher of our faith." Before it started, it was already done. The situation right now is not a surprise to God. It has not taken Him by surprise; therefore, you will come through! Your family, finances, and health will come through! Everything that belongs to you will come through! Today, you are taking everything back!

Say to yourself—I will not go down!

Say to yourself "I will not go down!"

I Will Not Give In!

The culture we live in wants you to give in. Winston Churchill said, "… never give in, never give in, never, never,

I Will Not!

never, never—in nothing, great or small, large or petty—never give in except to convictions of honor and good sense.[1]

> Therefore, as soon as they heard the sound of the horn, flute, zither, lyre, harp and all kinds of music, all the nations and peoples of every language fell down and worshiped the image of gold that King Nebuchadnezzar had set up. At this time, some astrologers came forward and denounced the Jews. They said to King Nebuchadnezzar, "May the king live forever! Your Majesty has issued a decree that everyone who hears the sound of the horn, flute, zither, lyre, harp, pipe and all kinds of music must fall down and worship the image of gold, and that whoever does not fall down and worship will be thrown into a blazing furnace. But there are some Jews whom you have set over the affairs of the province of Babylon—Shadrach, Meshach and Abednego—who pay no attention to you, Your Majesty. They neither serve your gods nor worship the image of gold you have set up."
>
> Daniel 3:7–12 NIV

In the above Scripture, we see three Hebrew boys pressured to give in to their environment's culture. They are expected to conform to the ways of the world's system and fit in.

I tell you that the only culture you need to build right now is the kingdom culture. That is the only culture worth building. Build it on earth, as it is in heaven. The Bible tells us to carry out God's will on earth "as it is in heaven" (Matthew 6:10). It is time to get active and pull some things down from heaven to earth to get things in motion. God can do His work on this earth through us as vessels.

---

[1] https://bit.ly/35zAtGJ

I Will Not!

> Shadrach, Meshach and Abednego replied to him, "King Nebuchadnezzar, we do not need to defend ourselves before you in this matter. If we are thrown into the blazing furnace, the God we serve is able to deliver us from it, and he will deliver us from Your Majesty's hand. But even if he does not, we want you to know, Your Majesty, that we will not serve your gods or worship the image of gold you have set up."
> Daniel 3:16–18 NIV

The Hebrew boys did not give in! They did not conform to the world's ways; instead, they stayed true to their faith. As a result of their commitment and steadfastness, the king came around and believed in their God. He later promoted them.

> Then Nebuchadnezzar said, "Praise be to the God of Shadrach, Meshach and Abednego, who has sent his angel and rescued his servants! They trusted in him and defied the king's command and were willing to give up their lives rather than serve or worship any god except their own God. Therefore I decree that the people of any nation or language who say anything against the God of Shadrach, Meshach and Abednego be cut into pieces, and their houses be turned into piles of rubble, for no other god can save in this way." Then the king promoted Shadrach, Meshach and Abednego in the province of Babylon.
> Daniel 3:28–30 NIV

Do you know that in the middle of chaos, you can receive a promotion? You do not know what God has in store for you. He has so much! He is waiting. At a time when you are

I Will Not!

not looking for promotion is the very time He says, "This is your time." He will promote you.

I Will Not Give Up!

If we are going to minister to lost souls and see a harvest, we cannot give up. In Luke 10:2 (NIV), the Bible says, "The harvest is plentiful, but the workers are few."

I would have given up 30 years ago when I started the ministry, but something in me said it is worth fighting for. David, who became king of Israel, offered a sacrifice to God and said in 1 Chronicles 21:24 (GNT), "I will not give as an offering ... something that costs me nothing."

In the middle of chaos, you can receive a promotion.

Today some people do not understand sacrifice. Hebrews 13:15 (NIV) tells us, "... let us continually offer to God a sacrifice of praise." A lot of the time, we do not want to give anything up. I am telling you that you must lay it all down, give it all up, and hand it all over for the sake of the Spirit of God having dominion in your life. When you begin to do this, watch what God will do for you because of your sacrifice.

Without sacrifice, there is no fire.

I Will Not!

Without sacrifice, there is no fire!

Without sacrifice on the altar of God, nothing can happen. We must realize that it is necessary to give up some things to serve God. It is hard, and it will cost you! Relinquish your control and let the Spirit of God take control of your life and watch what He will do.

Walt Disney went to bank after bank and was consistently turned down when he asked for money. He was looking for an investment to transform a swamp area into a theme park with a cartoon mouse—but he never gave up. Eventually, the Magic Kingdom was built along with the Epcot Center. The park was opened after his death, and people made the comment,[2] "What a pity Walt was not here to see it." However, Walt did see it, and that is why it is here.

Sometimes you must see through the eyes of faith. You may not see the result through your physical eyes, but you are not led by your physical eyes anyway. We walk by faith and not by sight. Learn to be led by the Spirit of God, not by your physical eyes—even when the odds are stacked against you.

Many of you reading this book could have given up many times, but you did not. You are still here. There is something remarkable in a man and a woman that perseveres.

"I will not give up" is the bottom line; God has given us a second chance. He has given everyone a second chance—even a third, fourth, fifth, sixth, and seventh. It does not matter what you have done, and it does not matter what you have gone through. You are loved. You need to know today that God has not given up on you, even though people may give up on you. Those you thought would believe and have faith in you may

---

[2] https://disneyparks.disney.go.com/blog/2010/05/a-moment-with-art/

I Will Not!

lose that confidence and give up on you. God does not change his mind; He never gives up on anyone!

I Will Not Let Go!

In Genesis 32:22–31, Jacob wrestled with God and said, "I will not let go until you bless me." Some of us have been believing God to save our friends or family and have become frustrated, and we are ready to give up, not knowing if they will ever be saved.

God is still asking: will you trust me? Do you believe that I am big enough? Do you believe that I can do what I said I would do?

The book of Acts 11:14 (ESV) says, "He will declare to you a message by which you will be saved, you and all your household." Therefore, we need to believe in the final product. We need to believe that God can do that which He promised.

Nobody has gone so far away that they cannot come to Jesus Christ. As a pastor, I went through a divorce. I never saw it coming or fully grasped what happened. I thought it was over for me. Growing up, I had the belief that ministry would end if you divorce or remarry. I didn't know what to do when I found myself in that situation.

The relationship that I needed the most was the same one that fell apart for me after fourteen and a half years. I said, "God, I do not know what I am going to do. I have lost the church that I started, a dream You put in my heart to plant."

I took a job at the local Starbucks, my favorite place. At the age of 38, I started working there. A big guy like me behind the counter, working with teenagers bossing me around, made for an awkward situation. They could make drinks and serve

I Will Not!

customers while I was still trying to look at the instruction book—trying to figure out how to make a non-fat decaf with an extra shot of foam. I said to myself, "I do not know how to do this."

Still, I kept going back. I kept waking up early and walking into the store at 4 a.m. to set up the pastries. One day, I realized that this is not for me. I knew this could not be God. After my three months of probation, I phoned the manager at the end of the shift and asked if I could meet with her. The next day I said to her, "You know, the last three months have taught me so much. It has taught me I am not made for this job." She said, "Well, that is good because we were about to let you go." I thought to myself, "Glory be to God!" It all worked in my favor. I was able to quit a job before being fired. Hallelujah!

However, I did feel like a failure. At 38, I couldn't even work at a Starbucks (being a barista is one of the most challenging jobs you could ever get!), but I still felt like a failure. Afterward, I got one job driving a dump truck for a landscape company and another cleaning local banks late at night. One day I said to God,

"You have not called me to do this."
He replied, "Yes, but I never gave up on you. You are the one that gave up on yourself."

I replied, "God, I am not going to let go till you bless me. I know your plan is greater, I know your plan is better, and I know that you were the one that called me, and not anyone else." It says in 1 Thessalonians 5:24 (NIV), "The one who calls you is faithful, and he will do it."

I prophesy over you today that if you do not go down, if you do not give in, if you do not give up, if you do not let go— the one who has called you and is faithful will do it! He

I Will Not!

will do what you could not do. He will love you and reach those souls around you that you thought you could not reach. He will bless you and restore you. Why? He loves you. You cannot do a thing to make Him stop loving you.

Maybe you feel like throwing in the towel. I understand, I have been there but look at Hebrews 13:5b (AMP), "For He has said, 'I will never [under any circumstances] desert you [nor give you up nor leave you without support, nor will I in any degree leave you helpless], nor will I forsake or let you down or relax My hold on you [assuredly not]!'"

God is with you! Do not give up!

"When God wants to bless you, he will bring people around you, and when God wants to protect you, He will take them away."

Pastor Frank Seixas

Chapter 3

Anywhere But Backwards

After my time at Starbucks, I made up my mind that I would not allow my experiences to dictate my future. I would not give in, throw in the towel, or quit! I have come too far with God not to allow Him to carry me through this period of my life.

I must leave it all behind and focus on what is ahead. There is no use in looking back, but there is so much to gain in looking forward.

You may have had to face some giants in your life, dealt with some difficult circumstances, or may have been kicked when you were down. Do not allow that pain, abuse, rejection, and disappointment to keep you from moving forward.

Don't be a prisoner of your past.

Anywhere But Backwards

The enemy of our soul wants to remind you of everything you have done and gone through so he can keep you as a prisoner to your past.

Philippians 3:12–16 (NLT) says, "I don't mean to say that I have already achieved these things or that I have already reached perfection. But I press on to possess that perfection for which Christ Jesus first possessed me. No, dear brothers and sisters, I have not achieved it, but I focus on this one thing: Forgetting the past and looking forward to what lies ahead, I press on to reach the end of the race and receive the heavenly prize for which God, through Christ Jesus, is calling us. Let all who are spiritually mature agree on these things. If you disagree on some point, I believe God will make it plain to you. But we must hold on to the progress we have already made."

Paul spoke compelling truths in telling us to not look back at the past but hold on and press toward our future. God still has good things in store for those who trust Him to lead them.

Do Not Look Back!

What happened to Lot's wife when she looked back (Genesis 19:26)? Nothing good. Many people have fallen into a destructive mentality, continuing to think about what happened to them in the past. They refuse to get over it because they do not want to stop living with the pain. They feel as though if they did, they would not have anything left.

That is not true. It is time to change our outlook and our focus. We need to get past our past and press forward. If we are going to move forward, we must look at what the Scripture says in 1 Thessalonians 5:16–18 (NIV) "Rejoice always, pray continually, give thanks in all circumstances; for this is God's will for you in Christ Jesus."

Steps to Moving Forward

1. Always be Joyful.

You might say, "But God, I do not want to be. I am not always joyful." Not many of us are always happy or joyful, but as we look at the word of God, there are so many places where God tells us to be joyful regardless of how we are feeling.

> Always be joyful in the Lord! I'll say it again: Be joyful!
> Philippians 4:4 GWT

> God, your God, has anointed you with the oil of joy beyond your companions.
> Hebrews 1:9b CSV

> This is the day that the LORD has made; let us rejoice and be glad in it.
> Psalm 118:24 ESV

> My lips will shout for joy when I sing praise to you—
> I whom you have delivered.
> Psalm 71:23 NIV

The oil of gladness and joy is available for you if you desire it. If you desire to be joyful despite your pain, heartache, and pressures of life—God has it readily available. You may have woken up this morning, and something terrible happened, or your day got off to a bad start—it is okay; just ask God for the Spirit of joy.

I remember telling God, "I cannot live up to that. I don't feel joyful. To always be joyful is not possible." Then I remember what the word of God says:

> You have shown me the paths that lead to life,
> and your presence will fill me with joy.
> Acts 2:28 GNT

Even when you do not feel joyful, God can still come and fill you with His joy. The Scripture tells us in Romans 14:17 that the kingdom of God is made up of righteousness, peace, and joy in the Holy Ghost. I see so many people walking around professing to be Christians, and some of them look like they have been baptized in pickle juice because they are so miserable.

Why would someone be drawn to you if you are always miserable? If you are around such people, you need to find others who can bring out the joy in you.

When we make God happy, the joy of the Lord fills us. Our goal on earth is to please our heavenly Father, but many are trying to please everybody else. It is only you and God when everyone else leaves. That is when you need the joy to begin to bubble up.

Always be joyful.

Anywhere But Backwards

All you have been through was not only for you in the first place; it was also for somebody else coming up behind you because God knows you would be able to help them get through what you went through. Our trials and tribulations are to help the next generation to overcome whatever challenges they face.

Two of the biggest problems in the world today are hunger and thirst. In Matthew 5:6 (NIV), it says, "Blessed are those who hunger and thirst for righteousness, for they will be filled."

How can you have joy in the Holy Spirit if you do not experience the Holy Spirit? We need to be filled every day. One of the greatest theologians, C. H. Spurgeon, was asked one day, "Why do we need to be filled with the Holy Spirit every day?" He said, "Simply because we leak." Every one of us has holes in us, and therefore we need to come before the Holy Spirit and say, "Holy Spirit, come and fill me afresh today. I cannot have what I had yesterday. Come and fill me, for it is not by might or power, but it is by Your Spirit." So many believers are spiritually dead because they will not allow the Holy Spirit to move.

He wants to fill you up so much that it is overflowing. It is flowing out of you just like the Bible says in John 7:38 (KJV) that "out of his belly shall flow rivers of living water." We are most fulfilled when we are doing what we are called to do and led by the Holy Spirit.

Have you ever been upset, disappointed, discouraged, and you didn't know what to do? I believe if you allow the joy of the Holy Spirit to fill and stir you up inside, it will restore you.

Anywhere But Backwards

But let the godly rejoice. Let them be glad in God's presence.
Let them be filled with joy.
Psalm 68:3 NLT

And the believers were filled with joy and with the Holy Spirit.
Acts 13:52 NLT

You turned my wailing into dancing; you removed my sackcloth and clothed me with joy.
Psalm 30:11 NIV

For the kingdom of God is not a matter of eating and drinking, but of righteousness, peace and joy in the Holy Spirit.
Romans 14:17 NIV

But the fruit of the Spirit is love, joy, peace, forbearance, kindness, goodness, faithfulness.
Galatians 5:22 NIV

Instead of your shame you will receive a double portion, and instead of disgrace, you will rejoice in your inheritance. And so you will inherit a double portion in your land, and everlasting joy will be yours.
(Isaiah 61:7 NIV).

We see from these and many other scriptures that joy is essential because it is mentioned in several places. The last Scripture gets me really excited, and hopefully, you too because God is setting you up. It says that you will possess a double portion of prosperity in your land, and everlasting joy will be yours. It is good to know that you can be filled with the Holy Spirit so that you can move forward.

2. Keep on Praying

The church is a house of prayer for all nations. God himself will fill you with joy as you pray, but sometimes I do not want to pray because it is too hard. We are told to pray. Isaiah 56:7 (NLT) says, "I will bring them to my holy mountain of Jerusalem and will fill them with joy in my house of prayer. I will accept their burnt offerings and sacrifices, because my temple will be called a house of prayer for all nations."

People are praying more worldwide than ever before. We have the International House of Prayer, Kansas City (IHOPKC), and many other prayer movements. We must believe that the prayers of God's people will penetrate the darkness and shift things so that we can see the mighty end-time revival that God has promised.

I have people who come to me and say: "Bishop, I want you to agree with me in prayer." "Okay, what are we praying about?"
"This and that."
"Do you believe it can happen?" "I am not sure."
"Well, I am not sure either."
Then, I walk away.

The Bible says in Matthew 18:19 (NIV), "… if two of you on earth agree about anything they ask for, it will be done for them by my Father in heaven." First, there must be the power of agreement for us to pray about your need. If you do not believe in it, surely, I am not going to believe in it, and if you do not believe in your God, surely other people are not going to believe in your God.

Faith and Prayer go together.

We have so many people praying but do not believe in what they are praying for, so their prayers are hindered.

The woman with the issue of blood in Mark 5:25–34 (NIV) said, "If I just touch his clothes, I will be healed." With that faith, she pressed through the crowd, and her faith touched Him before her flesh did. You cannot look at Mark 5 without looking at Psalm 133:1–2 (NKJV), where it says, "Behold, how good and how pleasant it is for brethren to dwell together in unity! It is like the precious oil upon the head, running down on the beard, the beard of Aaron, running down on the edge of his garments." Something happens when we get to the edge, which was known as the lowest point. This woman touched Jesus at the lowest point. The revelation here is: If you do not come under the head, you do not have the anointing. It said the oil of anointing went down the beard; the beard represents wisdom. You can have the anointing, but without wisdom, it means nothing. Then it went down his body to the edge of his garment, again the lowest part of the body.

In I Thessalonians 5:17 (KJV), it says, "Pray without ceasing." Or another translation says, "Keep on praying." That is the second way in which we keep moving forward. Isaiah 56:7 (NLT) says, "I will bring them to my holy mountain to Jerusalem and will fill them with joy in my house of prayer. I will accept their burnt offerings and sacrifices, because my Temple will be called the house of prayer for all nations."

One of the things in the North American church today that is missing is a heart for prayer. Many people from different countries that have come to Canada have been a great inspiration because I believe that God has brought them here to help us learn how to pray again. It appears we have lost that love for prayer that we once had before. Matthew 21:13 (NLT) says, "He said to them, 'The scriptures declare, "My Temple will be called a house of prayer," but you have turned it into a den of thieves.'" 2 Chronicles 7:14 (NLT): "Then if my people who are called by my name will humble themselves and pray and seek my face and turn from their wicked ways, I will hear from heaven and will forgive their sins and restore their land." If we truly seek Him and turn from our ways, then we will move toward what God really has for us to do. He will restore our land. Mark 11:24 (NLT) says, "I tell you, you can pray for anything, and if you believe that you've received it, it will be yours."

Believe inwardly before you receive outwardly.

How many times have you prayed, and you wonder if it is even getting anywhere? Do you wonder if it is getting past the ceiling? But today, I want you to know that if you pray, and if you ask, then you will receive. The Bible in Mark 11:24 (NIV) says, "Therefore I tell you, whatever you ask for in prayer, believe that you have received it, and it will be yours." You must believe it inwardly before you have it outwardly. If we believe inside our spirit man, it can manifest and come true in the natural.

Anywhere But Backwards

"Now this is the confidence that we have in Him, that if we ask anything according to His will, He hears us. And if we know that He hears us, whatever we ask, we know that we have the petitions that we have asked of Him."
1 John 5:14–15 NKJV

"Pray like this: Our Father in heaven, may your name be kept holy. May your kingdom come soon. May your will be done on earth, as it is in heaven. Give us today the food we need, and forgive us our sins, as we have forgiven those who sin against us. And don't let us yield to temptation, but rescue us from the evil one."
Matthew 6:9–13 NLT

"Don't worry about anything; instead, pray about everything. Tell God what you need, and thank him for all that he has done."
Philippians 4:6 NLT

When in a fix, Philippians 4:6!

There is something compelling about prayer. While I was in Bible college, my grandfather, Charles Gill, would send me little pieces of paper clippings from the Sunday school papers, and he would write on them. He always told me: "When in a fix, Philippians 4:6." I always remembered it.

Anywhere But Backwards

"Pray in the Spirit at all times and on every occasion. Stay alert and be persistent in your prayers for all believers everywhere."
Ephesians 6:18 NLT

I want to encourage you today to try and do that each day. I tell people that if they want to pray in their prayer language, try by starting off just five minutes a day. The next day, build it by increasing it to 10 minutes, then to 15 minutes, and then they will really begin praying in the Spirit. This is how we increase longevity in praying in the heavenly language. There has never been a greater need for prayer on this earth.

We fight our battles through prayer.

In 1999, there was a man named Mike Bickle in Kansas City. He felt that he had heard from the Lord to start a 24/7 prayer room for worship and prayer. It was to be open 24 hours, 7 days a week, 365 days a year. Mike shared this with people close to him, and they thought he was a little bit crazy. He believed. He knew that God had a plan for him and that He wanted him to do this. Mike went ahead and carried out the vision. He opened a building where people could pray every day. Today, in Kansas City, we have what is known as the International House of Prayer (IHOPKC).

IHOP operates 24 hours, 7 days a week, every day of the year. God is using it, and He is pouring out His Spirit. I have been to the IHOP twice, and it is incredible to see young adults mobilized from all over the world, giving their life to prayer. It is powerful to see people pray.

I recently had an opportunity to travel to Asia. While in Asia, I saw God move in a mighty way. My team and I were in a gathering, and as we were praying, there was a knock on the door. The authorities had come, and we were not sure what would happen, but God was with us, and everything went smoothly. It all happened as we were praying.

There are so many places in the world going through persecution and do not have the privilege to pray openly. Ephesians 3:16–20 (NIV) says,

"I pray that out of his glorious riches he may strengthen you with power through his Spirit in your inner being, so that Christ may dwell in your hearts through faith. And I pray that you, being rooted and established in love, may have power, together with all the Lord's holy people, to grasp how wide and long and high and deep is the love of Christ, and to know this love that surpasses knowledge—that you may be filled to the measure of all the fullness of God. Now to him who is able to do immeasurably more than all we ask or imagine, according to his power that is at work within us."

Don't stop praying.

Right now, God is doing great things through prayer in the underground churches in China, Vietnam, and other countries. He has many people, young and old, around the world being mobilized for prayer.

God is doing some exciting things. I want to encourage you to begin to pray each day. Pray in the Spirit and believe God to lead you.

"Let the message about Christ, in all its richness, fill your lives. Teach and counsel each other with all the wisdom he gives. Sing psalms and hymns and spiritual songs to God with thankful hearts. And whatever you do or say, do it as a representative of the Lord Jesus, giving thanks through him to God the Father."
Colossians 3:16–17 NLT

3. Be Thankful

Always be joyful, keep on praying, and always be thankful. This is the will of God in Christ Jesus concerning you.
1 Thessalonians 5:16-18 NIV

In a visit with my counselor, he said, "You know more people than anyone I know in the world. You need to go on the road and start ministering." Up until then I had always pastored and was an itinerant minister, but at that moment, I was thinking, 'Who will want some broken guy that can hardly keep his head up?' I walked out of his office, and 45 minutes later, I got a call from a pastor that was about eight hours away, and he said, "The Lord just spoke to me and told me I'm supposed to bring you in for a ministry weekend." I began to cry and think, 'God, you did not forget me.'

There is always a reason to be thankful.

Anywhere But Backwards

Twelve years later, I have traveled the world by preaching the gospel. I have seen many people healed and give their lives to Jesus. God has blessed me with a wonderful wife. I went from four daughters to seven daughters and five grandchildren. I could not have thought it. I could not have written it. I never planned to remarry. I was just going to do my best to raise my girls and to love God. I remember people would come and see me, and I would be so low. They almost had to pick me up off the floor; they had never seen me that way before. I was always full of life. I was always the one helping everybody. I then came to the point where I needed help.

Today, I am thankful. You may be thinking, how can you be thankful when you are going through challenges that you do not know how to get out of? It is tough, but then look at 1 Thessalonians 5:18–24 (NIV) that says, "give thanks in all circumstances; for this is God's will for you in Christ Jesus. Do not quench the Spirit. Do not treat prophecies with contempt but test them all; hold on to what is good, reject every kind of evil. May God himself, the God of peace, sanctify you through and through. May your whole spirit, soul and body be kept blameless at the coming of our Lord Jesus Christ. The one who calls you is faithful, and he will do it."

How do we stay faithful amid tough times? This is the question many of us struggle with. We have to keep believing that God has better things in store for us. He wants to help us more than we can even help ourselves. 1 Thessalonians 5:19 tells us not to *"stifle the Holy Spirit."*

One of the things I am very thankful for today is the person and the power of the Holy Spirit. I need Him, I can't do anything without Him, but I can do anything with Him.

Anywhere But Backwards

How can You be Thankful?

Here are some key verses that can help you maintain a thankful heart and attitude.

Enter His gates with thanksgiving and come into His courts with praise.
Psalm 100:4 NIV

I will extol the LORD at all times; his praise will always be on my lips.
Psalm 34:1 NIV

I will praise you forever, O God, for what you have done. I will trust in your good name in the presence of your faithful people.
Psalm 52:9 NLT

O God, you are my God; I earnestly search for you. My soul thirsts for you; my whole body longs for you in this parched and weary land where there is no water. I have seen you in your sanctuary and gazed upon your power and glory. Your unfailing love is better than life itself; how I praise you! I will praise you as long as I live, lifting up my hands to you in prayer. You satisfy me more than the richest feast. I will praise you with songs of joy. I lie awake thinking of you, meditating on you through the night. Because you are my helper, I sing for joy in the shadow of your wings. I cling to you; your strong right hand holds me securely. But those plotting to destroy me will come to ruin. They will go down into the depths of the earth. They will die by the sword and become the food of jackals. But the king will rejoice in God. All who swear to tell the truth will praise him, while liars will be

Anywhere But Backwards

silenced.
Psalm 63 NLT

That is why I can never stop praising you; I declare your glory all day long.
Psalm 71:8 NLT

Praise the Lord, for the Lord is good; celebrate his lovely name with music.
Psalm 135:3 NLT

One of the most significant ways that we can thank God is through our praise. Here are five ways and reasons we can praise the Lord.
Bless the Lord, O my soul; And all that is within me, bless His holy name! Bless the Lord, O my soul, And forget not all His benefits: Who forgives all your iniquities, Who heals all your diseases, Who redeems your life from destruction, Who crowns you with lovingkindness and tender mercies, Who satisfies your mouth with good things, So that your youth is renewed like the eagle's.
Psalm 103:1–5 NKJV

Let's unpack some of these verses:

#1 God Forgives!

In Psalm 103:3, David tells us that our God is a God:

"Who forgives all your iniquities,"

That's a pretty good reason. How many are thankful that Jesus Christ comes and lives in your heart and that he forgives your sins? I'm very thankful for forgiveness because if we weren't thankful, we'd have no place to go, we wouldn't have life. He forgave us and gave us a life that is abundant, full, and ultimately eternal.

#2 God Heals!

"Who heals all your diseases."

Somebody reading this is struggling with physical sickness or disease. Jesus Christ wants to come, and he wants to heal you. It says he healed all their diseases. That doesn't mean some of them. It doesn't mean just one or two were healed. It says all; everything and everyone that were sick were healed.

I want you to believe and for faith to rise in your hearts so that we can see people healed by the power of Jesus Christ. God heals! God delivers! God saves!

#3 God Redeems!

"Who redeems your life from destruction,
Who crowns you with lovingkindness and tender mercies,"

We need to praise God because He redeemed our lives from the pit. He loves you. He loves us all with an everlasting love. Is that not worth praising God for?

I don't know what you're going through today. I don't know what you have faced recently. All I know is that Jesus

Anywhere But Backwards

Christ still saves. We sang a song when I was growing up that said, 'I serve a risen Savior.[3]' I want you to know today that Jesus Christ is the only one that can save you. He's the only one that can come and free us from our sin so that we can have the assurance of eternal life.

If you are reading this book and you are not sure if you have a relationship with Jesus Christ, he is waiting for you to ask Him into your heart. So right now, wherever you are, say this prayer:

> *"Dear Jesus,*
> *I ask you right now to come and live in*
> *my life.*
> *To come and be my Lord and Savior.*
> *I thank you that you forgive my sins.*
> *I thank you for healing all my diseases.*
> *And I thank you, Lord, that my best days*
> *are yet to come in Jesus' name.*
> *Amen and Amen."*

If you have prayed the above prayer, welcome to the family of God!

#4 God Satisfies!

"Who satisfies your mouth with good things."

He is the God that is concerned about you. He cares about what you care about, and He satisfies your desires with

---

[3] https://www.hymnal.net/en/hymn/h/503

good things. That means good things are in store for you. In Psalm 84:11 (NKJV) the Bible says, "no good thing will he withhold from those who walk uprightly." So, if you love him, He's not going to hold back His love from you, but He is going to let His love flow through you so that you can be ministered to and then allow you to love others. The love of Jesus is going to flow through you, and you're going to be able to do great and mighty things for the sake of the gospel.

#5 God Renews!

"So that your youth is renewed like the eagles."

God wants to renew you today. He wants to renew your future from the lies the enemy has been feeding you with, but you have to make a choice, to go forward and not backward.

The enemy keeps trying to keep us from looking ahead by keeping us in the past, focusing on our mistakes. Still, you need to summon the courage each time to remind the devil of his future. Today wave goodbye to the past and decide to move forward no matter what.

Every day decide to keep going, step by step, little by little, move forward because your greatest days are still ahead of you. And God will do so much for you. As it says in Philippians 3:13–14 (NLT), "No, dear brothers and sisters, I have not achieved it, but I focus on this one thing: Forgetting the past and looking forward to what lies ahead, I press on to reach the end of the race and receive the heavenly prize for which God, through Christ Jesus, is calling us."

I encourage you, if you're struggling with your past, please give it to the Lord. You don't have to hold on to your

Anywhere But Backwards

past any longer. You can get free from that today in the name of Jesus.

So, when we praise the Lord when we begin to give Him thanks for everything He's done, that's when the Lord is ready to let us see significant breakthroughs.

Father,
We bless you, and our soul gives thanks to you, oh God.
Father, in the name of Jesus, I thank you right now that those reading this book will begin to receive their as they offer prayers of thanksgiving to you.
We praise you for the breakthrough.
We thank you that they're not going to look back anymore.
I break the past right now in the name of Jesus.
I thank you that their best days are yet to come.
I thank you, God, that You still have a plan for their lives.
I thank you, Lord, that the way ahead of them is paved by Your Spirit.
I thank you, Lord, that those who are led by the Spirit they are the sons and daughters of the Most High God.
Amen and Amen!

The way to keep moving forward is to stay thankful. Make up your mind to leave the past behind. The place for your life is anywhere but backward. Let God restore you.

Anywhere But Backwards

Bible School Graduation, 1993
Pictured with Mom & Dad
David & Sandra Gill

Greg and Grandpa Charles Gill

*"What God has done in the past, is a model and a promise for what he will do in the future.
Though, he's too creative to do the same thing the same way twice."*

Dr. James Allman, Dallas Theological Seminary

Chapter 4

God Will Restore You

In 1 Peter 5:6–10 (NLT), "So humble yourselves under the mighty power of God, and at the right time he will lift you up in honor. Give all your worries and cares to God for he cares about you. Stay alert! Watch out for your great enemy, the devil. He prowls around like a roaring lion looking for someone to devour. Stand firm against him and be strong in your faith. Remember that your family of believers all over the world are going through the same kind of suffering you are. In his kindness, God called you to share in his eternal glory by means of Christ Jesus. So, after you have suffered a little while, he will restore, support, and strengthen you and he will place you on a firm foundation."

There are things that God wants to do in our hearts so he can restore us, because we all have areas in our lives that we require healing and restoration.

The word restoration and restore means to receive back more than what you had initially. Have you ever had anything taken away from you or stolen from you, or you felt ripped off by the devil or ripped off by someone? Most of us have been to that place before.

God Will Restore You

The word of God tells us that His mercies are new every morning. And if His mercies are new every morning, then you must know that God has a new thing for you. You don't need to pray back the old things. If God's mercies are new every morning, why would you want back what you already had? Why want back the old if God has more for you?

There are many things that God wants to restore. He wants to restore your health, wealth, family, and relationships. God wants to bring things back around. The very thing that you may struggle with right now is the very thing that God may use to minister to someone else through your life.

God Will Restore You

The Bible says in 1 Peter 5:10 that after you've suffered a little, what will happen? God will restore you.

After going through what I described earlier, I didn't know what I was going to do. People would come around and tell me there is still hope. God will still use you, and in my mind, I'm thinking, "Yeah, right." I doubted what they were saying. I said, "Well, God, I don't know if you can use some divorced guy whose life is falling apart." Despite my unbelief, people kept coming to encourage me.

The place of rejection is where God will restore you!

God Will Restore You

God always has a way. The very place where I was rejected is where God used to restore me. I thought my dream was to pastor a church of 150 people, but instead, God has me pastoring the world. He opened the world for me to travel and minister to people and see them set free by the power of God. That's my God! He takes your wounds and turns them into worship. He's going to take your pain and turn it into praise. The very thing that you're going through that you think may be hard right now, after you've suffered a while; even though it's tough, even though it's hard, you have to prophesy to your future and say I'm going through in Jesus' name, I'm going to make it to the other side, I'm going to get to where I need to go.

God Will Support You

How many are thankful for that? Hebrews 13:5 (NIV) says, "Keep your lives free from the love of money and be content with what you have, because God has said, 'Never will I leave you; never will I forsake you.'"

My God's going to support you no matter what you're going through. He's going to use people to restore you. All you have to do is get connected. People want to do life with you, and God will use them to walk with you.

He uses people for a reason. Maybe you're driving down the highway, and you blow a tire, and somebody stops to help you put a new one on. Sometimes He sends people for a season. Maybe you're sick, and someone's there for you, helping you, supporting you through the sickness, and then after you're well, they move on. God can also bring support for a lifetime; these are covenant relationships that are with you for every journey of your life.

God Will Restore You

Not everyone will stay with you forever. You may have thought that person was going to be with you through everything. People come, and people go. God will support you, and God will bring people that will stand with you. Not everyone will be able to stand with you. Some may get tired, and others may tell you how bad your situation is or how bad you are. You do not need anyone to tell you how bad you are. The enemy does a good enough job on you himself. You just need to find people who will celebrate you and support you instead of tolerating you and put you down. Go where you are celebrated, not where you are tolerated.

Go where you are celebrated, not where you are tolerated!

God Will Strengthen You

2 Corinthians 12:9–10 (NIV) says: "But he said to me, 'My grace is sufficient for you, for my power is made perfect in weakness.' Therefore, I will boast all the more gladly about my weaknesses, so that Christ's power may rest on me. That is why, for Christ's sake, I delight in weaknesses, in insults, in hardships, in persecutions, in difficulties. For when I am weak, then I am strong."

Apostle Paul went through a lot of hardship, like us today, but he learned that when he's at his weakest is when he's the most powerful because of the strength of the Lord. Sometimes we sing "You are my strength when I am weak, you

God Will Restore You

are the treasure that I seek, you are my all in all"[4] and other amazing songs, but do we believe them? Because when we are at our lowest, he will take you to your highest. It is not about us. It's about him. It's about lifting up the name of Jesus. He will draw everybody to himself. You need to know that when you trust in him, he comes and strengthens you. You may not trust anybody else; that's okay. Learn to trust God and watch the miracles begin to happen in your life. God wants you to trust him.

God Will Establish You

God is about to set you up. What you thought was a setback is really a setup. Revelation 21:5 (KJV) says, "And he that sat upon the throne said, Behold, I make all things new." Jesus himself, the one sitting on the throne, says, look or behold, I am making everything new. He's restoring you. He's turning things over. He's turning things around in your life, making all things new for you. Look what it says in Ephesians 6:11 (NIV), "Put on the full armor of God, so that you can take your stand against the devil's schemes."

In tough times you need to learn how to stand. Psalm 62:6 (NLT) says: "He alone is my rock and my salvation, my fortress where I will not be shaken." I will not be shaken, see amid your circumstance, in the midst of what you're going through today, you need to stand, and you need to say I will not be shaken. You must be determined. All hell could be breaking loose around you, but you must decide that you're strong enough because of God inside of you. Job 42:10 (NLT) says:

---

[4] Dennis L. Jernigan- You Are My All in All. © 1990, Shepherd's Heart Music, Inc. (admin. PraiseCharts.com)

God Will Restore You

"When Job prayed for his friends, the Lord restored his fortunes." In fact, the Lord gave him twice as much as before! In verse 12, it says, "So, the Lord blessed Job in the second half of his life even more than in the beginning, for now he had 14,000 sheep, 6,000 camels, 1,000 teams of oxen and one thousand female donkeys." God blessed Job more in the second half than he did in the first. He gave Job double for his trouble after he had suffered a while.

God will restore you, he will strengthen you, he will support you, and he will establish you. He will do it. He has in store for you double for your trouble.

There is double (reward) for your trouble!

Chapter 5

Step into Your God-Given Destiny

After God restores you, it is time to step into your God-given destiny, and here are seven keys that will help you step into it.

Key #1 - Freedom

We need to exercise freedom. Galatians 5:1 (NLT) says this, "So Christ has truly set us free. Now make sure that you stay free, and don't get tied up again in slavery to the law."
I know so many people who are delivered and set free by God, but then they go right back into the same thing they were freed from. How many have been there, how many have had that happened in your own life? Probably many of us have. We need to make sure that we stay free. In Luke 13:12 (NIV), Jesus saw the woman with infirmity, and he called her and said, "Woman, you are set free from your infirmity."

Step into Your God-Given Destiny

1. Spend time in Prayer

To maintain your freedom, you need to pray. Prayer must be at the center of everything. Jude tells us to build ourselves up in our most holy faith by praying in the Holy Ghost. Invest in your prayer time. Ephesians 6:18 (NLT) says, "Pray in the Spirit at all times and on every occasion."

2. Get into the Word

To discover how much of the Bible you know, can you recite as many scriptures as your age? You cannot count John 3:16, Psalm 23, or "Jesus wept." from John 11. Other than those, how many other scriptures can you recite?

In 1989, when I was in Bible college, I got a call that my mom, Sandra Gill, had breast cancer. In my college room, I remember crying and saying, "Lord, I don't know how to deal with this. I've never had anybody close to me sick before." I opened my Bible and began to read the book of James. I learned the first chapter and memorized it to help me deal with my mom's sickness. Today I can attest that the word became real, and it took hold in my heart during my mom's illness. Twenty-seven years later, my mom is still living and well. Although it was a painful experience for her, she is still being used by God, ministering to women and raising money for missions.

If you are struggling in any area of life, search the scriptures for verses that apply to it. You can use the concordance in your Bible or go online to find Bible verses pertaining to your situation. There is a word for every situation we go through. Go to the scriptures and find answers from God that will help you overcome and have victory. You can also call a friend, an elder in the church, or even a pastor. They can assist you in your search and advise you on your dilemma, pray for you and with you.

3. Get involved in Ministry

In churches, 20% of the people do 80% of the work. If you want to step into your God-given destiny, serve. Find someone that is in worse need than you are and help them. Find a hurt and heal it. Find a need and fill it, and you will have a great ministry because I remind you there is always someone going through something worse than what you are going through. So, just find those people, and you will be fulfilled. Also, call your church or pastor, because I guarantee there are always things around the church that need doing and established ministries that need help. Try one to see if it fits. If it doesn't, try another, and keep trying until you find a fit. (Be FAT. Faithful, Available, and Teachable.)

Be FAT!

(Faithful, Available, and Teachable!)

---

4. Share your Faith

We need to make sure we're continually sharing the gospel with people. Everyone, according to the scripture, is called to do the work of an evangelist. It doesn't say you'll be a fivefold ministry evangelist, but it says you're called to do the work of an evangelist. So that means you need to open up your mouth and speak. You can't just say I'll let my light shine and people see it, but you also have to speak out by the power of the Holy Spirit. God has not given us the Holy Spirit so we can feel good. He gave us the Holy Spirit, so we can have the boldness to share the good news.

A psychologist once told me the number one thing that people are afraid of is public speaking, and because of that, they are afraid to share their faith. I want to nudge you a little and encourage you to just open your mouth. In Psalm 81:10 (ESV) the Bible says, "open your mouth wide and I will fill it." So, open your mouth, and the word of God will come out of you.

5. Keep the Pressure On

What do I mean by that? Just keep doing what you're doing. Some people think they need to change everything. Often, they don't need to change things. They just need the endurance to persevere through what they're going through. Romans 5:4 (NLT) says, "And endurance develops strength of character, and character strengthens our confident hope of salvation."

One of the greatest keys to the Christian life is perseverance. It's easy to keep going when everything's good, but how about when things are bad. When you're going through an attack, the easiest thing is to run back to where you're comfortable because the enemy wants to control you through comfort. But God says I want to take you like an elastic band and stretch you because I know that in the stretching is the making of man. He says I've come like the refiner's fire and I'll come, and I'll refine you, and you will come out like gold on the other side. Even though there is pain during the refining, it will be worth it, so keep the pressure on.

Key #2 - Faith

If we are going to step into our God-given destiny, we need to have faith. Faith is a confident assurance that something we want is going to happen. It's a certainty that what we desire will be right there when we need it. But by faith, we can already see it there. 1 Timothy 6:12 (NLT) tells us, "Fight the good fight for the true faith. Hold tightly to the eternal life to which God has called you, which you have declared so well before many witnesses." 1 John 5:4 (NIV) says, "for everyone born of God overcomes the world. This is the victory that has overcome the world, even our faith."

Faith says YES you can!

Faith says I can have it; you shall have whatever you believe for. The Bible tells us that "If you openly declare that Jesus is Lord and believe in your heart that God raised him from the dead, you will be saved." (Romans 10:9 NLT). The principle is true for everything. If we need healing in our body, we must believe in healing, and God can do it. If we need a financial miracle, we must believe that God will provide financially.

Step into Your God-Given Destiny

Key #3 - Focus

Focus creates a vision or a picture in our minds of how things could be in the days ahead. Hosea 4:6 "People perish for the lack of knowledge." I know someone has been waiting a long time for something to happen in their life, and as you are reading this book, I prophesy it shall come to pass in Jesus' name.

God's vision for your life is always bigger than your natural abilities. If you can do it on your own, then you probably know it's not God.

So, what do you do with a vision? You write it down. Habakkuk 2:2 says, (and this is my paraphrase) "Write down the vision, write down the revelation, make it plain and run with the vision."

When I was pastoring, people would tell me they had a great idea for the church. My response would always be, "Great! Go write it down and send it to me." Do you know that 90% of people never wrote it or brought it back? That tells me it couldn't have been that great an idea.

I've learned that when I write things down, that's when they start happening. If it is not written, it will not get done. Teachers always tell students to write everything down. That way, they can memorize and remember it.

Key #4-Favor

Favor is kindness and help rendered beyond what is due.
May the favor of the Lord our God rest on us, establish the work of our hands for us—yes, establish the work of our hands.
Psalm 90:17 NIV

Step into Your God-Given Destiny

> Surely, Lord, you bless the righteous; you surround them with your favor as with a shield.
> Psalm 5:12 NIV

Some people have specific graces in certain areas. For me, I have travel favor on my life. I remember one year before I had frequent flyer privileges, I had eleven free flight upgrades to business class. When I arrived at some hotels, the receptionist would say to me, "We've been waiting for you. We will upgrade you to a suite." When God favors you, nobody can do anything about it. God wants His best for you and wants you blessed. As you are reading this book, I speak the favor of God to follow you everywhere you go in Jesus' name.

I've had people come up and hand me money saying we want to bless you. There was a time a lady sitting beside me at a conference said, "Pastor, you ministered to me so much. For over a week, I've had this money in my pocket. I was going to buy a lottery ticket with it, but something kept telling me to hold on to it. I believe I'm supposed to give this $200 to you." I thanked her and believed that she would get a better harvest than a lottery ticket. We have to believe and declare the favor of God is on us.

Don't rely on what you see or what is happening around you—rely on the favor of God to work for you.

If you have ever felt that God doesn't want to bless you or that he's holding something back from you, I hope the above scriptures tell you otherwise.

Favor can change medical reports on your behalf; favor can change your pay rate and your job. Favor can restore relationships, and it can also give you a parking spot because

Step into Your God-Given Destiny

God cares about those things. If he cares about the birds, surely, he cares about me. Recognize the little things in your life and be appreciative of them all.

Everyday I expect favor. From your mother's womb, God has placed his hand on you. He has something in you that others can't see.

God's anointing will take you to the place of favor and authority so you can fulfill your assignment in life. Favor puts you somewhere at the right time; favor puts you before the right people at the right time. You don't know where God can put you. God can put you in front of things or presidents of companies. I'm telling you that not everybody is going to like you when you step toward your assignment, but long before others had an opinion of you, God had a destiny waiting for you.

For his anger last only a moment, but his favor lasts a lifetime.
Psalm 30:5 NIV

Here is a confession for you to say over your life every day and declare the favor of God.

I believe and confess that God's plan is to prosper me and not to harm me. God's plan is to elevate me and not to demote me because eye has not seen, ear has not heard, nor has it come into our understanding what God still has in store for me. For the Lord is giving me joy in all things, causing favor and blessing to flow toward me. The favor of the Lord goes with me everywhere, and the Lord's blessing is manifest even in adverse situations. God's favor to collect the goods from the wicked ones rests upon me. God's divine elevation in the sight of the enemy rests upon my life. The eyes of the Lord go with me and causes me to stand before kings and to have favor with all men. The favor of the Lord brings notice to my life in the presence of those who will bless and promote me. I believe and confess that the favor and honour, which will frustrate the enemy, has rested upon my life. The favor of the Lord, which brings me good understanding, is coming my way. I am receiving breakthrough ideas, which open the doors to help me confront the wrong and be favored with new understanding. I believe and confess that I will be patient until the day of my promotion. I confess boldly that the kindness of the Lord upon my life extends to the Heavens. God satisfies my mouth with good things. He took my mourning and gave me laughter, weeping may have been for a night, but my joy has come forth. The favor of God's anointing and strength is upon my life. It flows in me and causes me to rise above all situations. The favor, which follows a wise servant, is upon my life. I am blessed and highly favored.

Key #5 - Fire

We need fire to step into our God-given destiny. First, we need the fire that is in the word of God. Jeremiah 23:29 (NIV) says, "'Is not my word like fire,' declares the Lord, 'and like a hammer that breaks a rock in pieces?'"

Second, we need refiners' fire, Psalms 66:10 (NASB 1995) says, "For You have tried us, O God; You have refined us as silver is refined." Many of us don't like that because it hurts too much.

Third, we need the Holy Spirit's fire, as in Luke 3:16 NIV where it says: "John answered them all, "I baptize you with[a] water. But one who is more powerful than I will come, the straps of whose sandals I am not worthy to untie. He will baptize you with the Holy Spirit and fire."

Be around people on fire for God!

Four, we need the all-consuming fire of God. For our God is a consuming fire. We need to make sure that God consumes us and lights us on fire for Him. Many years ago, John Wesley said, "I set myself on fire and people come to watch me burn.[5]" When was the last time somebody saw you on fire for God, that they wanted the fire that you had?

I want to encourage you to get around people on fire for God, people who are hotter than you. I've learned the key to moving to the next level is to always find someone who's a little bit further along than you, rub up against them and get what they have so that what is on them gets on you.

Key #6 - Friend

In the book 'Taking Our Cities for God' by John Dawson, he said, "Find a friend to serve and discover your God-given destiny."

Your destiny is tied to somebody else. People are a gift of God to you, to get you to your destination. In Proverbs 17:17 (NIV), it says, "A friend loves at all times, and a brother is born for a time of adversity."

It is easy to stay with people when things are going well, but will you stay with them when it's going tough? We need each other all the time because at times you don't have the strength to fight by yourself and on your own. The church is

---

[5] https://bit.ly/2XxxRV4

called the body because everyone has a role to play in each other's lives.

Friends are important. 1 Corinthians 15:33 (NIV) says, "Do not be misled: 'Bad company corrupts good character.'" If you can show me your friends right now, I'll show you your future in five years. Your friends have a more significant influence on your life than your own family. So, it's crucial the choices we make when it comes to friendships. Everybody needs good and godly influence in their lives to help them stand strong and realize that they don't have to fight the battle on their own.

Key #7 - Forgive

We need to bring forgiveness back into our churches and our lives.

Colossians 3:13 (NIV) tells us, "Bear with each other and forgive one another if any of you has a grievance against someone. Forgive as the Lord forgave you."

One of the greatest things that hold people back from stepping into their destiny is an offense. Even worse is a second-hand offense. You pick up someone else's offense, and that goes down the line. Trouble always happens in churches when someone would get upset with a minister, and after telling their friend, that friend will take their side and get offended with the minister on their behalf. Let's forgive each other, so we can all fulfill our God-given destiny.

Chapter 6

Seven Steps to a Turnaround

I don't know where you're at today, but many of us probably need some sort of breakthrough in our lives.

Some time later God tested Abraham. He said to him, "Abraham!" "Here I am," he replied. Then God said, "Take your son, your only son, whom you love— Isaac—and go to the region of Moriah. Sacrifice him there as a burnt offering on a mountain I will show you." Early the next morning Abraham got up and loaded his donkey. He took with him two of his servants and his son Isaac. When he had cut enough wood for the burnt offering, he set out for the place God had told him about. On the third day Abraham looked up and saw the place in the distance. He said to his servants, "Stay here with the donkey while I and the boy go over there. We will worship and then we will come back to you." Abraham took the wood for the burnt offering and placed it on his son Isaac, and he himself carried the fire and the knife. As the two of them went on together, Isaac spoke up and said to his father Abraham, "Father?" "Yes, my son?" Abraham replied. "The fire and wood

Seven Steps to a Turnaround

are here," Isaac said, "but where is the lamb for the burnt offering?"

Abraham answered, "God himself will provide the lamb for the burnt offering, my son." And the two of them went on together. When they reached the place God had told him about, Abraham built an altar there and arranged the wood on it. He bound his son Isaac and laid him on the altar, on top of the wood. Then he reached out his hand and took the knife to slay his son. But the angel of the Lord called out to him from heaven, "Abraham! Abraham!"

"Here I am," he replied.

"Do not lay a hand on the boy," he said. "Do not do anything to him. Now I know that you fear God, because you have not withheld from me your son, your only son."

Abraham looked up and there in a thicket he saw a ram caught by its horns. He went over and took the ram and sacrificed it as a burnt offering instead of his son. So Abraham called that place The Lord Will Provide. And to this day it is said, "On the mountain of the Lord it will be provided."

Genesis 22:1-14 NIV

If we want to experience a breakthrough in our lives…

1. Listen to God

We need to listen when the Lord speaks. It's so important for us to train our ears and our spirit so when he speaks, we can listen.

Some people hear God audibly, and they can attest that it is God. Others may never hear the Lord audibly, and that's okay. That doesn't make you unspiritual. God can speak audibly, but He can also speak through His Word. Some may hear the Lord speak through a prophetic word. Sometimes we're trying to hear from the Lord with only our ears, but even more, I'd encourage you to hear the Lord with your spirit.

> "For those who are led by the Spirit of God are the children of God."
> Romans 8:14 NIV

How do we hear by the Spirit?

Sometimes you feel a prompt in the heart, just like in Acts 15:28a (NIV), "It seemed good to the Holy Spirit and to us." Now, I know some people won't like this, but I don't pray about every decision I make because not everything needs to be prayed about. You have to trust the Holy Spirit in you.

Some things seemed good to me in the Holy Spirit, so I acted on them. If it seems right in my heart, and I have a witness, I just act on it; I go with it. Some may say, "Well, that's not spiritual. You didn't hear from God." You do not need to hear God on everything. If I'm led by His spirit, then I know when the inner witness from the Lord speaks to me, and I can make decisions easily.

2. Trust God

We need to learn to trust the Lord just like Abraham did when God spoke to him to go to a place he'd show him on the way. We all need to get to the point in our lives where we come to the place where we sense the will of God.

Seven Steps to a Turnaround

Abraham trusted God without knowing where he was going. Although God told him, I'll let you know when you get to the place I am taking you. I don't know about you, but that's a very scary thing because, in our North American society, we want every "i" dotted and every "t" crossed, everything in line, and in order before we make major decisions. Can I suggest to you something new today? A man of God told me one time, "What we need, is we need spontaneity within the structure." It's not a bad thing to have structure, but we also need to leave room for the Holy Spirit to speak, move, and direct us.

Trust in the LORD with all your heart, and do not lean on your own understanding.
In all your ways acknowledge him, and he will make your paths straight.
Proverbs 3:5-6 ESV

Can you imagine if we all behaved and trusted like Abraham, going out there, not knowing where he was going? He was close to the mountain, but he wasn't on it. He had to rely on God to show him where to go. You and I, my friend, need to rely on the Holy Spirit to show us where to go.

Some people have a hard time trusting the Lord because they do not trust other people. And so, when trust is broken, it's hard to allow it back in. If there is no trust, there cannot be a true relationship. To build trust is to open up to one another. When God gives you a word, and you have a strong sense of what He is saying, allow yourself to trust Him.

Seven Steps to a Turnaround

3. Separate Yourself

If we're going to have a turnaround in our lives, we need to separate from the rest, though it says in Genesis 22:5 (KJV), "And Abraham said unto his young men, Abide ye here with the ass; and I and the lad will go yonder and worship, and come again to you." There are some places God wants to take you by faith that requires you to separate from others.

When you get close to your destiny, you will have to leave some people behind at times. In thirty years of ministry, I've learned that the people who started with you don't always finish with you.

Abraham was getting ready to go up a mountain, and then he tells his servants, "You stay there, and I'm going to go up the mountain." He tells the ones closest to him to stay put because the next phase was for him alone. Are you at a place where God wants to speak to you? If so, He may want you to separate from others, from friends, family, and the systems and break out because they're not called to do what you're called to do. They're not called to go where you're called to go. There should be no offense, hostility, or issues. It's just time for you to go to the next stage of your life, ministry, business, by yourself.

> "And everyone who has left houses or brothers or sisters or father or mother or wife or children or fields for my sake will receive a hundred times as much and will inherit eternal life."
> Matthew 19:29 NIV

4. God Has a Better Plan

We need to be thankful for what we have and make sure that we understand that God has a good plan. Not only obstacles can hold us back, at times it can be people. That's why you have to make sure when God speaks that you're not trying to be a people pleaser because your goal in life can't be to make everybody happy.

I remember a friend telling me he was waiting to be voted on to become a pastor of a local church, and if he didn't get 100% of the vote, he would not accept the position. I asked him what he thought about the scripture that says, "Woe to you when all men speak well of you." (Luke 6:26a NKJV). In the end he didn't accept the position because of the votes. You cannot allow what people think about you to determine the decisions you make in life. If we're doing something for God, then usually things will come against us, and that's a good sign that you're on the right track.

5. Be Willing to Sacrifice

After you've set everything up, you need to be prepared to sacrifice something that you love. Just like Abraham, when he said, "I'm going to sacrifice my son." Fire will not fall if there's no sacrifice. The miracle doesn't happen if there's no sacrifice. If your sacrifice doesn't move you, it certainly will not move God.

How much are you willing to give up to serve the Lord? There has to be a sacrifice. We used to say that we bring the sacrifice of praise into the house of the Lord, but what does it cost to bring that sacrifice? Many times we show up to meetings and struggle to sing, lift our hands, or dance in the presence of God, but the Bible says in Hebrews 13:15 (NKJV), "let us continually offer the sacrifice of praise." That means even when you don't want to do it. Why? Because the sacrifice you're giving is yourself!

6. Be Ready for a Switch

To switch means the ability to turn things around in the middle of a situation. Abraham lifted the knife, and the angel stopped him, and God switched things around for him.

Where are you at? What do you need switched in your life? You may be stepping toward something that all of a sudden God says "Switch!" If you need a breakthrough in your life, I'm telling you, you need to go right over to that light switch in your house right now, flip it, and just yell, "Switch!" and believe, in Jesus' name, that something's going to switch in your atmosphere.

7. God Will Provide

The Bible says Abraham looked up and there in a thicket he saw a ram caught by its horns. Like how the ram was tied up in a thicket, God has something tied up right in front of you. It's there. It's waiting for you. When the devil says no, God says yes. There is always a substitute because God always provides.

There were many times in my life where I didn't know where the next provision was going to come from, and I had to trust God. Sometimes I connected my faith with other people, and the power of agreement made a difference. Today, I am

Seven Steps to a Turnaround

thankful that the Lord brought me out of some dark places and allowed me to step into my turnaround and my season of overflow and abundance.

Greg and Diana Gill

Chapter 7

Time for Overflow and Abundance

It's your time for overflow and abundance. This next season of your life is going to usher in new things because your greatest days are yet to come.

> The thief comes only in order to steal and kill and destroy. I came that they may have and enjoy life, and have it in abundance [to the full, till it overflows].
> John 10:10 AMP

God has a plan for you to live a life of overflow and abundance, and it starts with the decisions you make each day—make a decision when you wake up in the morning what kind of day you want to have before you get out of bed and your feet hit the floor. I have a friend from Bogota, Colombia, who told me that every morning when he gets up, he decides that before his feet hit the floor, he's going to read his Bible—because he's hungry. So, if he doesn't read his Bible before his feet hit the floor, he doesn't eat breakfast. He said, "If I can't feed my spiritual hunger, I'm not going to feed my physical hunger." Every decision shape our future. Our decisions yesterday got us to where we are today, and our decisions today will determine our tomorrow. If we want tomorrow to be different from today, we need to make sure we make the right decisions. When I was seven years old, I gave my heart to the Lord at a camp meeting at Lakeshore Pentecostal Camp. Since that day, I've never turned my back on the Lord. For over forty years, I've served the Lord; it's all I've ever known. That one decision determined my life today.

The overflowing and abundant life also includes you owning your stuff and not blame someone or something else. We need to accept responsibility in life, so we can get wisdom. You can't have anointing without wisdom. Luke 2:52 (NIV) says, "And Jesus grew in wisdom and stature, and in favor with God and man." If he could grow in wisdom, then so can I.

> A wise man will hear and increase learning,
> And a man of understanding will attain wise counsel,
> Proverbs 1:5 NKJV

How do we get wisdom? First, from the word of God. James 1:5 (ESV) says "If any of you lacks wisdom, let him ask God, who gives generously to all without reproach, and it will be given him."

Second, from making mistakes. Sometimes, you have to learn the hard way.

Third, by other people's mistakes, those are much better.

Fourth, we invest in ourselves. I have a friend who flew from the US to a conference in Australia because there was a speaker there he felt he needed to hear that would unlock something in him. How many have ever gone to a meeting because you knew there would be something that would change your life?

My friend spent almost $12,000 USD traveling to the conference and bought a copy of every one of the speaker's materials and resources because he wanted to invest in himself.

He knew something was there. He got home, started listening, reading, and watching all the materials, learning valuable lessons from each one. While listening to one of the materials, an idea came to him that generated an income of $300,000. Investing in those materials triggered something that released him into financial abundance and overflow.

> You will be enriched in every way so that you can be generous on every occasion, and through us your generosity will result in thanksgiving to God.
> 2 Corinthians 9:11 NIV

We're blessed to be a blessing. Don't be manipulated to give because someone wants you to give but give so that you can be generous on all occasions.

The only reason we should want to get to the place of superabundance is so we can give and bless others. I remember I went through a stage that the Lord spoke to me that I should put something in the offering every time an offering was collected. That was stretching me because it's not every time I have the money. I asked God what happens if I don't have anything? And he replied, you find it because there's something that is activated when you sow a seed. So, I decided I'm going to respond generously. I know some who say we should not give so we can receive, but why not? The Bible says give, and

Time for Overflow and Abundance

it shall be given to you, so that means if you give, it's going to come back to you. For the measure you use, it will come back to you. If you want to experience the abundance and overflow, learn to respond generously.

> Surely, LORD, you bless the righteous; you surround them with your favor as with a shield.
> Psalm 5:12 NIV

> For his anger lasts only a moment, but his favor lasts a lifetime.
> Psalm 30:5a NIV

Chapter 8

Testimonies

I met Bishop Greg Gill over 15 years ago at a youth group under Pastor Warren Beemer, whose leadership I currently serve. He immediately became a voice of ministry in my life. Throughout my walk with the Lord, he has witnessed both intense battles as well as victories, and the Lord has used his prophetic voice greatly in my life. I appreciate the gifting that Bishop Greg carries and honor him as one of my spiritual fathers. He is a launching pad for the kingdom of God and has not only impacted my life but so many others around the world. It is an honor to walk as a spiritual daughter with Bishop Greg and even the more to exhort you in reading his book *I WILL NOT!* It's a good day!

Pastor Jen Diaz
Third Day Generation

    I met Greg in what would have been the darkest, most desperate time in my life. I had been suffering from depression and suicidal tendencies as a result of PTSD, memories of sexual abuse as a child, and making some really bad life choices that had hurled me right into the middle of a divorce. I was somewhat homeless, broke financially, broke spiritually from a not-so-graceful exit from my church of almost 20 years. I had gone from being well respected in church leadership to an outcast in the blink of an eye. There was little hope for me to hang on to, and I was beginning to get to a place where I didn't care to "remain" on this earth any longer. However, there was a steady and strong longing to hang on to Jesus with everything I had. It was literally a back and forth battle every day.

    I had inched my way into a small church in Boerne, Texas, where the pastor was a very good friend of mine, and quite frankly, one of a handful that stood beside me and walked with me to try and make it through to the other side of this season. I had read where this "pastor from Canada" was going to be visiting our church. I can remember sitting at work and coming to the conclusion in my mind that I didn't have any interest in going to listen to this man preach because it was my pastor who was walking me through my healing, and I didn't "need" to listen to another person. However, that wasn't in God's plan for me. For the next four days, I fought God about going to listen to Bishop Gill preach.

    I woke up that Sunday morning with every intention of doing "internet church," but the Spirit of God kept hammering me to get up and go to church. So that's what I did, very reluctantly. I walked into the sanctuary and talked with a few people, then went and took my normal seat: 2nd row on the right, end seat. The worship that day was so good, and I just resigned myself to this being a good day and being open to what God wanted to do.

    As Bishop was introduced and he took the mic, I started to feel an excitement in my spirit, much like when you are

Testimonies

waiting to see something or hear something that God had for you individually. As he began to speak, he said the topic of his sermon was, "The Rest of Your Days are the Best of Your Days," and I just locked onto his words with tears welling in my eyes the whole sermon. I just remember the Lord saying to me over and over, "Son, this isn't the end … trust me with this new beginning." I was walking in such shame over everything that was going on…the things that I had caused for other people … how awesome was it that God sees past that to encourage us in a new life even when we burned the last one down. As the sermon when on, I felt like I was the only one in the room that was being preached to. I was the only one he was addressing. And I noticed he kept looking at me.

As he began to close, Bishop stopped what he was saying, and I could tell the Lord was speaking to him. There was a heaviness of the Holy Spirit in the room; I just couldn't stop crying because I knew I was supposed to be here for this word today. He raised his head, and I could see tears on his face, and he turned toward me, pointed his finger at me, and said, "Come here!" It was a little humorous because one of the associate pastors stood up, and Bishop said, "Not you! The guy behind you!" I stood and walked up to where he was, and you could have heard a pin drop. Bishop then began to line out every single thing I had been going through in detail. There is no way, other than God, that he could have known the things he spoke because they were things I had never told anyone … not even my pastor. He answered questions that I had been asking God and God alone. Then he said this, "God sees your need where it comes to finances and your future. The reason you have nothing right now is because what you had was corrupted. God has an incorruptible call on your life, even in light of your failures, but you cannot take what's corrupt into the incorruptible call. You aren't broken. You're just being made incorruptible for the rest of your days, and what God's pressing you into will be mind-blowing. I'm weeping uncontrollably at this point, then he puts his hands on me and says, "REST!". The next thing I remember is laying on the floor knowing the Holy Spirit had just taken my fears, my guilt and shame, and my failures and given me a hope for the future. I was able to sit with him after church and talk for quite a while, and he encouraged me right out of my hole.

I was able to go to a church leadership meeting that night, and Bishop was there. As I walked into the room, he looked over and shouted at me, "Hey, Hammer! Good to see you on your feet!" From that day, Greg and Diana have been such dear friends to my God-given wife, Denise, and me. Every single thing Greg prophesied over Denise and I have come true, without exception. We are serving in ministry today, just as he prophesied. We were ordained as ministers of the Gospel, just as he prophesied, we would. We are better for all he has poured into us and are also equipped to pour those same things into others who are struggling.

Chuck Ham
Huntsville, AL

I met Bishop in 2017 in our local church, led by Bishop Joey in Beijing. Actually, that was the first time I heard the title "Bishop." I was curious what a bishop looked like and their role. However, through the conference, all my curiosity about the title was forgotten since what he shared and taught about the Holy Spirit was fascinating, the power in speaking in tongues, etc., there were not only new learning about God and

His Word, but I also felt freedom through bishop's teaching. I knew that God had used his message to set me free and minister to my soul and spirit.

I'm always so grateful to see foreign ministers, like Bishop Greg, who come to China to bless us and our country. I see his big heart and love for people here. May God bless Bishop Greg and his ministry.

Sophia Du
Beijing, China

I met Bishop Greg Gill in Aug 2017 through a ministry friend that we both knew, Pastor Warren Beemer. On that specific morning, fetching Bishop Greg Gill from Cape Town International Airport, we had a divine encounter. We did not know each other, but something in our spirits just leaped. I could sense God's anointing presence from the very first moment we connected.

That morning, my wife and I, together with one of our leaders, drove him to the hotel. When we arrived at the hotel, Bishop could not check in until later because his room was not ready. This turned out to be a setup by God Himself.

We decided to have breakfast at the hotel, and what transpired in the next few minutes was God's divine intervention. Bishop Greg began to speak into our lives exactly what we were feeling, what we were going through, and where we found ourselves.

As we were sitting, it felt like I just got an epiphany that created a nuclear reaction in my life. Everything turned right there at the table, there was this fresh wind of God blowing, and Bishop Greg just continued speaking into our spirits.

Testimonies

This day turned out to be a day where God used an ordinary person in an extraordinary way. To think God would send a man halfway around the world to cross the Atlantic sea just to let a young couple in ministry know God is not done yet. Our tears were flowing. How could this be? This man whom we just met me knew what we were going through. He became known as the connector, the Bishop of Bishops, the pastor who pastors leaders. This man just became the light in a dark tunnel by just saying it's not time to give up. He prophesied about things that we just prayed for just that morning. It was like everything around us was fading away, and we could just dwell in God's presence. The rest, they say, is history.

We began to develop a relationship, and I became part of Ignite the Nations International Network becoming the Overseer over South Africa. With my whole heart, I believe that every leader needs a leader like Bishop Greg Gill, who will blow life back into every dry valley and begin to speak life. This man became the epitome of a great leader.

Pastor Alvin Olivier
Rock City Church Cape Town

I met Bishop Greg Gill in 2019 for the first time in Bangkok, Thailand, when I served there as a missionary. We were connected through a mutual friend in Australia who had said that when Bishop Greg had come to Australia, he made a huge impact on his life. We talked a few times online, and I found that he had already planned to come to Bangkok. This would be my last month in Bangkok as my family was planning to move to New Zealand.

Testimonies

When I picked him up from the hotel in Bangkok, I took him for dinner, and I wanted to tell him that I wouldn't be able to arrange many meetings for him at this time, my family was preparing to move to New Zealand, and it was a busy time. I felt sad that I would not be able to do many meetings for this great man of God. When we got to the restaurant, and I told him about this, I thought that he would be sad and discouraged that he had come so far and wouldn't be able to have many meetings while here in Bangkok. I was touched and surprised by his reaction, which came from love and a relational heart, He said, "If I only met you and went back, I'm happy." This man was different, most only want meetings, but this man wanted to build relationships.

On Saturday, during our regular church service, he preached the word of God. This was the first day I served together with this man. I could feel the anointing of God over him and the wisdom he carried to share the word of God with others. I still remember while I was interpreting, I cried a few times. His message was touching and encouraged us to keep moving forward, our church was blessed, and everyone was saying how timely and touching this message was.

After that day, we started to build our relationship more and more. We started to communicate every week. This was a changeable season for me and my family as we moved to New Zealand right before coronavirus and the lockdowns of 2020. Through all of this, he remained faithful. He encouraged me to do media ministry during this season, and I have been doing this since April. It has been a blessing reaching thousands, mostly in India and Pakistan. When we decided to plant a church in New Zealand, he encouraged us in this move, not only with words but with actions.

I have connected with him from the beginning of Ignite Ministries, and I'm part of the team. I can see that he has encouraged so many through this network and his life. He walks with a gift of encouragement, not only in words but in actions and faithfulness. This book, *I WILL NOT!* will bless and encourage many and lift people up in their walk of faith.

Pastor Mark Amir
Auckland, New Zealand

It is my distinguished privilege to participate in and contribute in any small way to Bishop Greg's book project.

What can I say about the Bishop!! He is truly a gift to the Body, a gift to the people who gather "In the River" (that's the name of the local assembly where my husband and I pastor), and he is a gift to my family and me in a very personal way. We thank God for him.

The Bishop and I met at a time of great uncertainty and challenge in my life and the life of the church, where I then had the honor of assisting my pastor, Pastor Nelson Sammy-Guilarte, Living Word Christian Center. There was a weekly, two-hour, live TV program which I co-hosted with my Pastor and at the time of Bishop Greg (he wasn't a Bishop at the time) coming to Trinidad and being invited to be on the telecast that week. My Pastor had gotten seriously ill, and I was thrust into a situation of having to host the program alone. Now for anyone who has sat as a co-host on a program and then having to suddenly host, knows that there is a vast difference between

Testimonies

following the lead and leading yourself. So that was the context in which we met for the first time.

Bishop Greg was so very gracious and encouraging that we 'flew' through the two hours, and the Holy Spirit ministered mightily through him to the nation. Praise God!!

Since that time, January 2011, even though we didn't see each other for the next seven years, the Bishop consistently reached out to my husband, my family, and me via all the various platforms of keeping in touch -text messages, WhatsApp, calls, etc. He is such an encourager!!

The outcome of any form of communication with Bishop ALWAYS resulted in us being built up (literally), encouraged (literally), and exhorted to keep going forward and going deeper in God (literally)!! He calls peoples' destiny out of them!!

We went from being brand new acquaintances to having a brother and sister-like relationship even though we didn't meet again face to face until he returned to Trinidad as part of an evangelistic team in August 2018.

He graciously agreed to minister at our church in response to a very impromptu invitation, I might add, and POW!! Holy Spirit showed up at that meeting in such a mighty way!! The house has never been the same again!! Glory to God!!

My husband, Robin, and I are thrilled that we get to be a part of the Ignite the Nations International Network!! The core values of this Network -Relationship, Empowerment, Honor, Generosity, and Contending for the presence of God are a description of the heart of its founder and leader, Bishop Greg Gill.

Testimonies

As you read this book, may these qualities of Christ in the Bishop be imparted to you.

Pastor Michelle Ramcharan
Trinidad

Chapter 9

New Mindset

I've come a long way from the broken marriage, working at Starbucks, and feeling as if my life and ministry were over. God gave me the strength, courage, and support I needed to say I WILL NOT!

I will not go down, even though there are giants in my life!
I will not give in–in the commotion—there is a promotion!
I will not give up–because God never gave up on me!
I will not let go – there is a blessing in holding on!
I refuse to look back!
I choose to move forward by being joyful, prayerful, and thankful!
I know God forgives! God heals! God redeems! God satisfies, and God renews!
God will restore me!
God will support me!
God will strengthen me!
God will establish me!

New Mindset

Today I choose to step into my God-given destiny by freedom, faith, focus, favor, fire, friendship, and forgiveness!
I will experience a turnaround as I listen to God, trust Him, separate myself, sacrifice, and switch!
He will provide for me because He has a better plan!
This is my season of overflow and abundance!
Because
I WILL NOT!

For more information about Bishop Greg D. Gill
visit www.myeim.org

I WILL NOT!
Pursuing the Path to Perseverance

Bishop Greg D. Gill